DOING DEALS

A Guide to Buying Land for Conservation

DOING DEALS

A Guide to Buying Land for Conservation

written by
The Trust for Public Land

published by
the Land Trust Alliance, Washington, DC,
and The Trust for Public Land, San Francisco, CA

Printed in the United States of America.

First printing.

For information, contact the Land Trust Alliance, 1319 F St. NW, Suite 501,
Washington, DC 20004-1106.

This publication is designed to provide accurate, authoritative information in regard to the subject matter covered. It is sold with the understanding that the publisher is not engaged in rendering legal, accounting, or other professional service. If legal advice or other expert assistance is required, the services of competent professionals should be sought.

Doing deals: a guide to buying land for conservation / Trust for Public Land.
      p. cm.
    Includes bibliographical references and index.
    ISBN 0-943915-11-2 (alk paper)
    1. Land use—United States. 2. Nature conservation—United States.
    3. Land trusts—United States. 4. Real estate investment—United States.
    I. Trust for Public Land (U.S.)
    HD205.D65 1995
    333.73'16'0973—dc20   95-10136
                                                         CIP

Cover, text design, and production: Judith Barrett Graphics
Printing: BookCrafters, Virginia
Printed on recycled paper

Contents

Preface

In 1988, the Trust for Public Land and the Land Trust Alliance joined forces to publish *The Conservation Easement Handbook,* the seminal publication on how to protect land through conservation easements. With *Doing Deals: A Guide to Buying Land for Conservation,* we are proud to offer a companion volume that provides practical guidance on land trusts' other major land protection tool: land acquisition.

The Trust for Public Land (TPL) and the Land Trust Alliance (LTA) are dedicated to helping communities preserve land. For over twenty years, the Trust for Public Land has conserved our nation's fragile landscape by acquiring more than 1,200 parcels of land and conveying them into the protective ownership of public land management agencies and land trusts. One of its founding missions is to share its expertise with the American land trust community, and it has played a role in the establishment of more than 300 land trusts.

The Land Trust Alliance is the national organization of land trusts. Since 1982, the Alliance has provided land trusts with information, training, publications, and technical expertise. As leader of the fast-growing land trust movement, LTA guides its development through programs such as the Land Trust Standards and Practices program and National Land Trust Council, educates the public about land trusts, and advocates public policies that help conserve land.

This book is a distillation of TPL's experience working with and training community groups to undertake land conservation acquisitions. It is based on training materials developed for TPL's National Land Counselor Program (NLCP), which provides intensive training for land trusts in land acquisition techniques.

Nelson Lee, TPL vice-president and general counsel, wrote the case studies and provided editorial oversight of the project. Heidi Hopkins, NLCP manager, developed the manuscript, managed reviews, and coordinated TPL's role in the book project as a whole. Ernest Cook, senior vice-president, contributed hours to the project as a primary expert and reviewer. Elizabeth Byers, land trust program director in TPL's Western Region, and Steve Thompson, senior vice-president, reviewed the book in its entirety. There are many, many more TPLers whose experience and writings over the years appear in this book. We are deeply grateful for their contribution.

The Land Trust Alliance proposed the joint publication of this book as a way to make the excellent materials and training developed for the NLCP available to the land trust community and other conservationists. LTA assisted in determining the book's content, structure, and approach, and managed the publication process. Karen Deans, LTA director of publications, edited the book and oversaw production.

Eight land trust experts generously gave their time to review the manuscript's first draft. These include: Sylvia Bates, director of land protection for the Society for the Protection of New Hampshire Forests; Thomas Bradbury, president of the Kennebunkport Conservation Trust; Story Clark, director of protection for the Jackson Hole Land Trust; Janet Diehl, project manager for the California State Coastal Conservancy; Thomas Duffus, director of conservation programs for the Adirondack Land Trust; Sam Gusman, board member of the Taos Land Trust; Elizabeth Hagood, formerly executive director of the Lowcountry Open Land Trust and NLCP alumna; and Rand Jack, attorney and board member for the Whatcom County Land Trust.

TPL and LTA would like to thank the following funders for contributing to the publication of this book. Providing funding to TPL: the David and Lucile Packard Foundation, Geraldine R. Dodge Foundation, Claneil Foundation, Friendship Fund, Inc., California State Coastal Conservancy, and others who wish to remain anonymous. Providing funding to LTA: the Fund for the Preservation of Wildlife and Natural Areas, Lennox Foundation, Marpat Foundation, Inc., National Fish and Wildlife Foundation, The Strong Foundation for Environmental Values, and Sweet Water Trust. TPL and LTA are very grateful for their support.

Jennie Gerard
Senior Vice-President
The Trust for Public Land
February 1995

Jean Hocker
President
Land Trust Alliance
February 1995

Chapter 1

INTRODUCTION

Across the country, hundreds of non-profit land trusts are protecting land, using a variety of protection methods. This book is about one of land trusts' essential conservation tools: buying land.

Sometimes land trusts will buy land because they want to—buying land gives the greatest control over its use. Sometimes they buy land because they have to—perhaps sale is the only option the landowner will consider. Regardless, buying land is a tool that every land trust must know how to use.

ENTERING THE WORLD OF REAL ESTATE TRANSACTIONS

Buying land puts the conservationist into the world of real estate transactions, a world that seems mysterious, sometimes harsh, with a vocabulary and style of its own. What is the "income approach"? Who pays the real estate broker? And what is all the fuss about "environmental liability"? For those experienced with conservation easements, many of these concepts will be familiar; for others, most of them will be new.

This book introduces the basic real estate, finance, and strategic principles that will enable the conservationist to operate competently and comfortably in the world of buying and selling real estate. Its goal is not to make every land trust practitioner an expert in such arcane areas as real estate appraisal or title law. It does not provide an in-depth examination of funding for land purchases —a book-length subject in itself—nor is it intended to be a comprehensive legal treatise. Rather, it will suggest a methodology, giving the land trust project manager enough basic information to:

- develop a strategy for acquiring a property

- pull together all the information necessary to understand the project and the players

- understand the process and feel comfortable working within it

- know when to seek help and how to effectively deploy others

While the focus of this book is acquisitions, many of the real estate principles and strategies presented here apply to the range of conservation techniques.

Using this Book

Following two introductory chapters, this book is divided into four sections.

Assembling the Information Chapters 3-7 describe information you'll uncover and activities you'll engage in as you research the project. What are the resources of the land? Who's the landowner, and what is his relationship with the land? Does your land trust have the staff and budget to pursue this at all? Might a public agency be interested?

Strategy and Negotiations Chapter 8 explains how to gain site control of a property, and discusses development of a final strategy and action plan. Chapter 9 describes the early stages of negotiations, and Chapter 10 focuses on putting the agreement down on paper. Chapter 11 describes the final steps in completing a project.

Due Diligence Steps Chapters 12-15 explain in depth title issues, surveys, hazardous waste assessments, and appraisals.

Paying for the Property Chapters 16 and 17 give an overview of the financial side of acquisitions, with information about interim financing and permanent funding.

The book can be read straight through to gain an understanding of the process, or used chapter-by-chapter as a reference.

Accept the Risk

Risk is integral to the business of saving land. In virtually every project, the land trust faces a certain degree of risk—financial risk, legal risk of contaminated property, or risk of negative public perceptions and reactions. Yet if a land trust doesn't put its resources and reputation on the line, it won't achieve its goals. The more a land trust can accept risk—even the risk of failure—the more it will achieve.

If there is any message this book seeks to convey, it is that risks can be managed, putting conservation land acquisitions within the grasp of any land trust. You have the commitment and the dedication. Take the principles and strategies laid out in these pages, and use them to guide your energies and passions. Good things will happen.

Chapter 2

APPROACHING A PROJECT

A project begins the moment your land trust first considers a piece of land for protection. This might be a property brought to your attention by someone familiar with the land trust's purpose and goals, one valued by the community that has suddenly become threatened, or one the land trust has identified in its long-range plan as important to acquire.

Regardless of how you become interested in a property, your first thoughts about your protection goal, in essence, begin the design for the project.

THRESHOLD DECISIONS

This book assumes that your land trust will have made certain basic decisions about a project.

The project is appropriate for your land trust. This is your starting point. You have decided that you know enough about a property and circumstances surrounding it to conclude that it should be considered for protection and that the project appears to be appropriate for your land trust.

Buying the land—or a partial interest—is probably the best way to protect the resource. You have decided that purchase of the property is the best means of protection, after which the land trust may:

- own and manage it

- own it while another entity (such as another nonprofit group or a public agency) manages it

- resell it to a third-party owner (such as a conservation buyer or a public agency)

- arrange a limited development

FRAMEWORK FOR YOUR APPROACH

Answers to certain fundamental questions provide the framework for your initial approach to acquiring a property:

- Is the land available (maybe it's not for sale)?

- What will it cost?

- How long do you have to put together a deal?

- Where will the money come from?

These focus you on an initial protection goal, and help you decide what to do first and who to involve (and when and how).

Early on in a project, you gather just enough information to identify critical issues and establish parameters that guide—or at least narrow down—further research. You're looking for the best information that can be reasonably obtained within time and money constraints. (Chapters 3-7 present the basic areas you will research, and Chapter 17 outlines a variety of potential funding sources.) As you research specific issues in greater depth, look into various funding possibilities, proceed with negotiations, and test your ideas with others whose expertise you can trust, you may revise your strategy or even change your protection goal. With experience, you will gain a sense of how much research you need to do at any point in the project, when to call in the experts, how best to use your available time (you never have enough), and how to quickly develop fallback strategies in the heat of a crisis.

Working on projects takes patience, flexible thinking, and common sense. It is not a linear process, nor are there formulas. It can take years, and the end result may be a successful preservation effort that looks nothing like what you originally envisioned.

A Winning Team

Any land trust taking on projects needs people who together can form an intelligent plan for protecting a property and can carry it to completion. This team of experts—attorneys, real estate brokers, bankers, and planners, working pro bono if possible—helps a land trust pull together the range of skills needed to achieve the protection goal while minimizing the risk. With the right team, a land trust can take on projects that at first glance might seem beyond reach. Over time, you and your team will develop the experience that will be your best guide, allowing the land trust to go toe-to-toe with the most sophisticated real estate professional.

BASIC PROTECTION METHODS

Deciding on the best method to protect the land is the first step in solidifying your project design. Although this book focuses on acquisition, your early considerations will, of course, extend to the full array of protection methods, used singly or in combination. (See Appendix A, "Conservation Tools and Strategies.")

Own and Manage

The most straightforward project is an outright fee simple acquisition (that is, acquisition of all the rights to a piece of land and of title to it) by the land trust, either by purchase or by accepting a donation. This puts the land trust in full control of the property. However, there is usually a high up-front cost and a continuing cost (and liability) of managing the land in perpetuity.

Own and Other Manages

In some cases, the land trust can acquire title through a fee simple transaction and simultaneously develop a management agreement with an appropriate manager, such as another nonprofit group or a public agency. This saves the land trust long-term management costs and responsibility. The key issue here, aside from the cost of the land, is structuring a sound management agreement that meets your protection goals.

Resell to Third Party

Some properties can be protected by acquiring them and reselling to a suitable third-party owner and manager. Although sometimes the third-party buyer is found after the land is purchased, often the buyer is involved from the start; the trust acts as an intermediary, negotiating with both the landowner and the buyer.

Many land trusts cultivate contacts with individuals or organizations that may be interested in purchasing scenic or open space property and are willing to accept use restrictions. Such a buyer might be an individual seeking land for a quiet home (frequently referred to as a "conservation buyer"), a farmer willing to purchase land restricted to agricultural use, or a nonprofit whose purposes mesh with your own, such as a group interested in running an ecological preserve for public education and research. Generally, it isn't easy to find such buyers, nor are they always legally obligated to restrict the land.

A land trust also can "preacquire" land for a public agency. Although preacquisitions can be complicated, their appeal is that they efficiently leverage public dollars available to preserve and manage open space. (See Chapter 7, "Agency Preacquisition.")

Limited Development

Sometimes portions of the property can be developed without sacrificing the protection goal. Such limited developments usually entail developing the less environmentally sensitive portions of a land parcel and selling these to a private buyer; the portion of the property with the most valued resources may be retained by the land trust or sold to a third party with conservation restrictions. The land trust may work closely with a developer or may act as the developer, managing the market analysis, planning, permitting, and building of the project (a very difficult undertaking). The advantage of this kind of project is that the development subsidizes protection of the rest of the land. On the other hand, developing land is time-consuming and extremely complex; the financial risks are usually high; and it invariably requires professional expertise. Perhaps more critically, the public perception that the land trust is developing rather than protecting land can damage its reputation.

Acquire Partial Interest

Owning real estate may be thought of as owning a "bundle of rights" that may be divided or shared in almost limitless ways. There is a range of opportunities for a land trust to protect land by acquiring, through purchase or donation, only one or a few of the rights. For example, if a farmer needs the land only as a hayfield for his cattle, you might offer to purchase the land with the landowner retaining the haying rights. If the land's resource value is likely to be damaged by mining but otherwise will probably be left in its current state, you might purchase just the mining rights.

Acquisition of a partial interest is usually less expensive than buying the land, and it can be acceptable to a landowner who is unwilling to part with the land.

Conservation easement. The most well-known means of conveying a partial interest is through a conservation easement. When a landowner sells or donates a conservation easement to a land trust, she agrees to restrict the type and amount of development that may take place on her land, and the land trust accepts the responsibility of monitoring compliance of the landowner and future owners. Conservation easements are never simple to draw up. All the careful research, thinking, and legal documentation that is required for fee acquisitions needs to be applied to easement transactions. In fact, in many respects an easement acquisition is more complicated, because the landowner and land trust need to carefully negotiate a unique set of rights and restrictions over the property, which in most cases will be in force forever.

As described earlier, a land trust may also buy land and resell it to a third party subject to use restrictions or may preacquire an easement for a public agency. (See *The Conservation Easement Handbook*, Land Trust Alliance, 1988.)

Other partial interests. There are other forms of partial interests that can be acquired to protect a property, such as:

- *Use rights.* Including mineral, timber, or water rights (as well as rights conveyed through conservation easements).

- *Deferred interests.* These include remainder interests (usually used in an arrangement in which the landowner sells or donates land to the land trust but retains the right to live on the land).

- *Partial undivided interests.* Land ownership typically becomes increasingly fragmented as land is passed from parents to children. Usually, ownership is divided among the inheritors, who become "tenants in common," owning equal percentages of the whole property (equal partial undivided interests). It may be relatively inexpensive to purchase a small partial undivided interest from one of several inheritors, and if you own such an interest, you can effectively prevent unwanted development or otherwise negotiate with the rest of the owners. But on the flip side, the other owners can prevent you from, say, building a trail or otherwise managing the land as you would like. You also will have partners, which can hamper any decision making.

Other Preservation Techniques

There are important preservation techniques you should be aware of that do not require land acquisition and may not, in fact, call for the active involvement of a land trust, except in an advocacy role.

Transfer of development rights. In some parts of the country, it is possible to acquire development rights through government "transfer of development rights" (TDR) programs. This is a complex mechanism and not widely used at present. Put simply, city or county planning bodies can establish areas designated for additional development and areas designated for no development. Someone wanting to build in the areas designated for new development must purchase development rights from a landowner owning land in an area where development is restricted. When development rights are sold from a property, permanent restrictions are imposed on the property. Land trusts can advise or administer such programs: they know the prime conservation areas and are familiar with the valuation of development rights, they are in a position to market the concept in the community, and they understand the acquisition process.

Zoning ordinances. Zoning provides an effective way to regulate land use. Land trusts can be active in sponsoring zoning laws that promote open space. (See "Land Use Planning," a special issue of *Exchange*, Fall 1990.)

Property tax reduction programs. Some states have programs that offer property tax relief to landowners who agree to limit the use of their property to activities such as farming or forestry.

Restrictive covenants. Used in many subdivisions, these regulate the use of property for the benefit of neighbors. They usually are enforceable only by the landowners involved and their heirs and successors.

Management agreements. Land trusts can work with landowners to establish a voluntary land management plan designed to achieve conservation goals.

Section I

ASSEMBLING THE INFORMATION

Once you've decided that you'd like to pursue a property, you begin a process of information gathering and analysis — about the land, the landowner, potential partners, sources of funding, and so on.

You'll probably follow these lines of inquiry simultaneously, exploring each to the degree demanded by the project and reacting to opportunities and roadblocks as they arise.

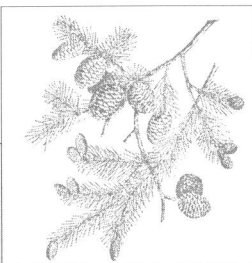

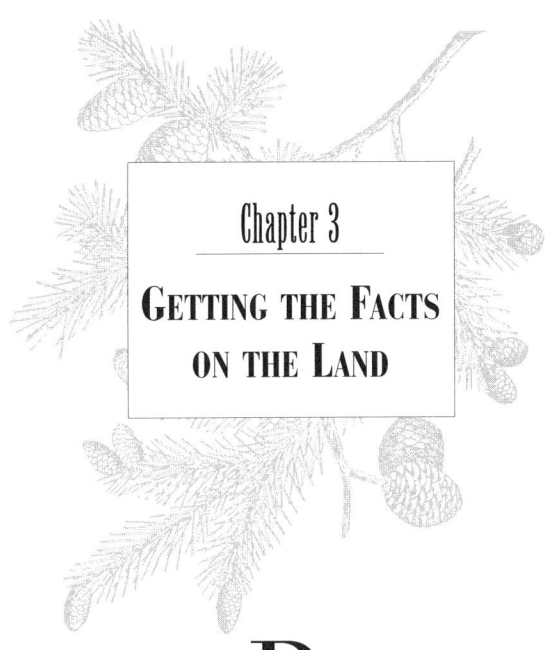

Chapter 3
GETTING THE FACTS
ON THE LAND

Buying land is risky business. With so much money at stake, with value determinations so imprecise, and with legal issues so complex, the buyer truly needs to beware. Your best safeguard is to know the land you're planning to buy. Familiarize yourself with its geographic features and resources; learn about its history; consider its relationship to current land use trends; find out whether there may be title or other legal problems.

How exhaustive your research needs to be will depend on the circumstances of your project, the amount of risk, and your land trust's time and money constraints. Do what you can within the limits of practicality (and remember to call upon the members of your land trust's team—realtors, planners, and appraisers).

The first question your land trust will want to ask is whether the property's resources are the kind your land trust was established to protect. Is protection of these resources consistent with your land trust's goals and purposes? Do the resources meet your selection criteria? You should not proceed with a project unless the answer to these questions is "Yes." (See *Developing a Land Conservation Strategy: A Handbook for Land Trusts,* Adirondack Land Trust, 1989.)

INSPECTING THE SITE

The best way to start learning about the land is to walk it, preferably with the landowner. See the land's features with your own eyes and hear about the land from someone who knows it.

Undertake the following steps for every site inspection (compiled from the Land Trust Alliance's *Standards and Practices Guidebook*):

- Get the landowner's permission.

- Prepare before visiting the site by reviewing any pertinent information you have about the property.

- Choose the time of year (if possible) so you get the information you want.

- Inspect key features, property boundaries, and survey markers. Do this with the landowner if possible.

- If the property is too large to walk or drive, supplement the ground inspection with an aerial inspection (or review aerial photographs).

- Record your inspection on a standard evaluation worksheet (the *Standards and Practices Guidebook* provides sample worksheets).

- Visit the site more than once.

Sources of Information

You can find much of the information you'll need about the land from the following sources:

- first-hand site inspection

- family members, neighbors, and local residents who use the land (keeping in mind that they may have their own reasons for wanting or not wanting you to buy the land)

- title reports

- existing appraisals

- recorded surveys

- property records, including property deeds, assessor's parcel maps, and recorded documents, such as leases or easements

- environmental assessments on the subject property or adjacent land

- plant and animal inventories by universities, state natural resources departments, state natural heritage programs, or conservation organizations

- agency planning studies (there are innumerable agencies that will have planning studies, from local water quality management districts to federal agencies, such as the U.S. Forest Service or the Army Corps of Engineers)

- county general plans

- environmental impact reports

- development proposals

- USDA soil surveys

- USGS topographical maps or aerial photos

- Government Land Office maps of early patents and lots

Inventory buildings and look for potential public hazards. Improvements such as homes, sheds, or mine shafts typically can be time-consuming and expensive to maintain. Buildings may need to be razed because they will interfere with resource protection, pose too much of a liability, or, in a preacquisition, because the agency cannot accept land with improvements. Natural features such as cliffs or lakes can be public hazards that greatly increase potential liability. (See "Land Trust Liability and Risk Management," George [Rock] Pring, *Exchange,* Winter 1991; this article also is a chapter in the *Standards and Practices Guidebook.*)

Whether or not you plan to allow public use, find out whether public access is physically possible and whether public use—either planned or uninvited—might pose liability or management problems. Ask the landowner and neighbors about historic public use of the land and about any access easements that may have been granted to neighbors or others. When walking the property's boundaries, look for adjacent public roads and evidence (such as trails or ATV tracks) of public use. Note anything that might make managing the land a problem. Are keg parties a possibility? Do people camp on the land, making fire a potential problem?

Look for indications that the property may have been contaminated by hazardous waste. Question the landowner and inspect the site to determine whether, for example, fertilizers, chemicals, or fuels may have been stored there. (Before purchasing the property you will need to do a comprehensive and careful determination of potential hazardous waste problems. See Chapter 14, "Environmental Assessment.")

Site Inspection Checklist

The critical things to look for include:

- source of physical access to the property
- type, significance, and condition of conservation resources
- threats to the resource, both on-site and off-site, such as a "For Sale" sign on adjacent property
- existing land use and intensity of activity
- improvements (buildings and other structures) and their condition
- safety hazards, both natural and structural
- public use problems, such as a fence that clearly is broken down by trespassers
- evidence of hazardous waste problems both on the site and on adjacent property (see Chapter 14)
- adjacent land use that might negatively affect the resource
- property boundaries

Developing Baseline Data

An initial site inspection may give you enough information to decide to proceed with a transaction, but if your land trust intends to hold and manage the property, you need to do a thorough review of the property's resources and document these as baseline data. This is usually done soon after the project closes. The level of detail needed in your analysis will depend on the type of resource you intend to protect and on the conservation plans for the property.

Documenting conservation values includes off-site research of existing data and on-site inspections, often by resource specialists, in which you will examine the kind and condition of water resources, natural habitat, agriculture, open space, and aesthetic and cultural features. Combining on- and off-site information and reconciling any differences should provide the most current and accurate site information.

SIZE AND PHYSICAL CHARACTERISTICS

Knowing a property's size and physical characteristics will help you:

- more accurately estimate the value of the property

- analyze the relation of the property's boundary to that of the resource to be protected

- identify encroachments, improvements, or public hazards that might complicate the project or compromise responsible stewardship

- estimate short- and long-term property management costs

- identify access points to the property

- determine whether the property is large enough to protect the resource and whether future development of adjacent land will negatively impact the resource

You need to know:

- What is the exact acreage?

- Where are the property boundaries?

- Is the resource to be protected included within property lines?

- Are there encroachments on any of the property's boundaries?

- What is the topography; e.g., are portions of the land too steep to develop?

- What is the configuration of the resources on the land; e.g., which portions of the land are timbered, which include wetlands?

One useful tool for answering questions of size and boundary location is a survey. Ask the landowner whether a survey of the property exists and whether you can see it. Check county records or local surveying firms for recorded surveys. Surveys generally are expensive, however, and not worth ordering in the early stages of a project. (See Chapter 13, "Survey.")

DEVELOPMENT CAPACITY

"Development capacity" refers to the practical and legally allowed uses of the land—its development potential. Development capacity is determined by the land's physical characteristics, relationship to adjacent land, existing deed restrictions or third-party rights, access to development infrastructure, and the current legal and regulatory framework. Analyzing capacity helps you determine desirable (and allowable) protection strategies. For example, it will help you predict development of adjacent land that might adversely affect your protection efforts or analyze the feasibility of a limited development. It also will solidify your negotiating base by helping you know what the actual threat is to the land, determine the realistic potential for development, and estimate the market value of the land.

Exactly how development capacity will impact the property's value is something that only professionals—brokers, appraisers, experienced project managers—can determine, though you will develop your own sense of this through experience. How it will affect your protection strategy depends on what uses you plan for the property. Be aware that there could be extremely high hidden costs: the purchase of water rights needed to restore a wetlands or keep a farm in production, the negotiation of an access easement across neighboring land for public access to the protected site, or a time-consuming and perhaps controversial subdivision approval process in the case of a limited development.

To determine development capacity, investigate the following issues.

Land use regulations. Find out what zoning and subdivision laws affect the property. The best way to learn about local land-use regulations is to talk to planning department staff and examine city or county general plans and related maps, which are available in the respective planning departments. In your discussions with department staff, be sure to ask how common it is for variances to be granted. (You could also ask the county supervisors, commissioners, or city council members.)

Both zoning and subdivision laws can change, of course, and are subject to exemptions and variances. Therefore, while (for example) the county general plan and zoning ordinance may clearly designate a property as open space, you need to assess the strength of that designation by considering:

- local politics, especially changes in politicians

- exemptions allowed on neighboring land

- local economic and development trends overall

In addition to local regulation, a variety of state and federal regulations protect wetlands, coastal areas, river corridors, and other resources. These usually are incorporated into regulations enforced at the local level; local planning department staff should be able to explain which state or federal regulations apply. (See "Land Use Planning," a special issue of *Exchange*, Fall 1990.)

Access to utilities and water. If the land lies miles from roads or power lines, or if its topography makes it impossible to connect with them, its development potential will be restricted. How much this affects value, and whether this is relevant to your particular protection strategy, is different in each case.

Lack of water or water rights can also greatly limit a property's use and value. In the project's early stages, rely on what the landowner tells you regarding water rights and availability. If water rights are critical to your protection strategy, however, you may have to turn to experts for help. (See Chapter 12, "Title.")

Physical and legal access. Physical and legal access is, of course, critical to developing a property. Check the property during your site visit for physical points of access and review any existing surveys or title reports. Check with the planning department to determine whether access permits are required from local, county, or state highway departments. This will be particularly important if public access is a requirement for your protection strategy.

Likely Cost of Owning and Managing Land

If you plan to hold the land for any length of time, find out all you can about what the costs will be. These may include insurance premiums, costs associated with building maintenance and repairs, utilities, and easement monitoring. There may also be significant one-time costs such as demolishing a building, removing old cars, or fencing in a riparian area.

Investigate current property taxes and due dates, which you can find in the assessor's records. Ask whether there are any assessments against the property for which the land trust may be liable or whether there are special use overlays (such as open space, flood plain, farmland, timberland) or deferments. If there are, will any penalty tax be due upon acquisition or disposition? You also can ask the agency that administers the special assessment program.

If you will be holding property intended for agency repurchase, you will need to maintain or enhance property values; for example, maintain access, keep development permits in place, and keep improvements in good condition and insured. If you don't, the value of the property might fall and you might end up losing money on the project.

Carefully thinking through what may be required and investigating costs and income potential will help you accurately assess your overall acquisition costs; estimate your interim holding costs or ongoing stewardship costs (and income); and estimate the landowner's financial burden, which may influence his negotiating position.

Managing land can be every bit as complex as buying it. A land trust that expects to hold land for any length of time should develop a short- and long-term land management plan. If you cannot foresee raising the funds necessary for adequate ongoing management, you should not take on long-term ownership of a property. (See "Managing Conservation Lands," a special issue of *Exchange*, Fall 1989.)

Identify Income Possibilities

Of course, land and its improvements may offer your land trust income possibilities. You may be able to rent out a building, lease a field to a neighboring farmer, or charge user fees for access to a beach or a system of recreational trails. (However, find out whether charging fees will eliminate your immunity to liability for recreational use.) You might lease fishing rights or cross-country ski trails. Surplus funds can be used to pay for the financing of a purchase of the land and can play a significant role in your project strategy.

Finding Unexpected Income

The Upper Buttes Land Trust had eyed the McLaren Ranch for years for its unequaled wild bird habitat along Quail Creek. Suddenly, Dave McLaren was ready to sell, but at a price comparable to what developers would pay him. The trust estimated it could raise half the purchase price through local fundraising, and borrow the rest. But how could it cover the interest costs on the loan and repay the principal when due?

The answer came from a trust sponsor who was an avid duck hunter. Why not put the part of the ranch with the best habitat value in a preserve, and lease the balance for seasonal rice farming and hunting? He pointed out that hunters were accustomed to paying top dollar for hunting rights for their "clubs."

After a long and complicated process the trust received approvals to subdivide three parcels on the periphery of the central preserve. It leased them both to farmers for the rice growing and harvesting season and to hunting groups, with severe restrictions on the hunting privileges. The income from the farm and hunting tenants met payments on the loan and funded a reserve sufficient to pay off the loan when it was due.

CURRENT AND PROJECTED LAND VALUES

The value of a piece of property is estimated through a subjective analysis of the property's size, shape, and terrain; its access to roads and utilities; applicable land use regulations; development and land value trends (what a buyer will pay) in the area; restrictive easements or covenants; and improvements on the land. Valuing land should be left to professional appraisers. Your responsibility is to know enough about valuing land to estimate the value of a piece of property and how it might change over time, know when to call in an appraiser, and evaluate an appraisal report.

Information on Value

The following sources of information can give you a shirt-tail analysis of the land's value before you invest in an appraisal:

- **Landowner.** Ask whether a recent appraisal exists that the landowner is willing to share. Ask how much the landowner paid for the property and whether the land is used as income property. Find out whether there are current, verifiable offers to purchase the property.

- **Realtors.** Ask realtors about prices paid for comparable properties in the neighborhood.

- **Assessor's office.** Find out from the assessor's records what the current assessed value is and in what year it was assessed, and whether assessed values bear any real relationship to appraised values in the area. (Note that, in some states, assessments are updated annually and generally reflect current market conditions. In other states, assessments are often well below market value.)

- **County recorder's office.** Value information can also be found indirectly through the tax stamps on the last deed recorded for the property, reflecting the purchase price for the property.

Over time, experience will sharpen your own ability to estimate value.

Do You Need an Appraisal?

Appraisals, while extremely useful, may be unnecessary. If a landowner is donating a piece of property or an easement, you don't need an appraisal (although the land trust has to value the property somehow for accounting purposes). Under IRS regulations, it is the landowner's responsibility to get an appraisal if claiming a charitable tax deduction. Ordering an appraisal simply to feel comfortable with price discussions early in negotiations may be an expensive luxury. (See "Alternatives to a Formal Appraisal" in Chapter 15, "Appraisals.")

You should order an appraisal when:

- your land trust will pay for land or an easement and there is uncertainty as to the property's fair market value (it is your fiduciary responsibility to justify your purchase price, in particular, when there is any possibility that you are paying more than fair market value, which constitutes "private inurement")

- your land trust intends to sell property to a private individual (an appraisal is essential to preclude charges of private inurement) (See *The Back Forty*, May/June 1991)

- you are dealing with a government agency that requires an appraisal

- the project is large, its are issues complex, or it involves a high degree of financial risk

- you are dealing with a landowner whose asking price is too high and who seems willing to agree to a more reasonable price if presented with objective value estimates

What Is the Market for the Land?

The value of the land is what someone will pay for it. A landowner may think her property is worth a million dollars, but if the market is dead, this value may be meaningless. Observing the market—how long properties are on the market, what the financing opportunities are, whether property sales follow long-term economic trends or fluctuate regularly with the seasons—will tell you what's really happening to land in your area. This knowledge is one of the most powerful tools you can have, helping you assess the true threat to the land, the landowner's alternatives, who your competitors are, and how much time you have to act.

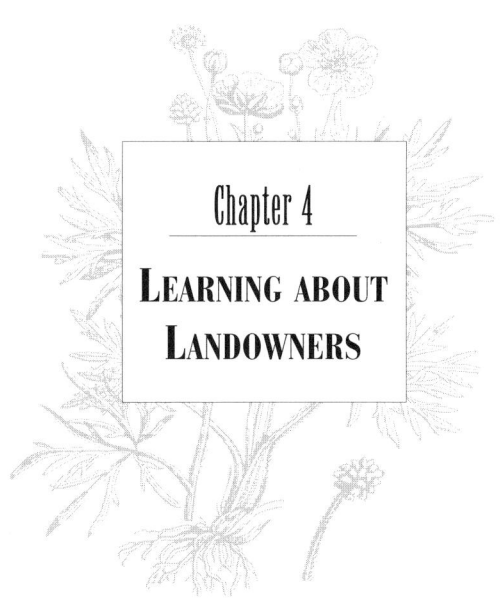

Chapter 4
LEARNING ABOUT LANDOWNERS

The landowner is your partner in a project. Your land trust helps the landowner dispose of land; the landowner offers your land trust a protection opportunity. This relationship may be kept strictly to business or it may develop into a long-term friendship, with the landowner sending projects your way, recommending you to others, or supporting you as a member or donor. Developing a personal relationship with the landowner and working toward a mutually satisfying goal can make a successful conservation project even more rewarding.

In the earliest stages of a project, you need to find out everything you can about the landowner's goals and constraints in order to plan your approach to negotiations and determine the best way to pursue a working relationship. What do you need to learn? The landowner's character, personal background, social and professional affiliations, current financial circumstances, relationship to the land—all of these can influence decisions about the deal.

This chapter describes landowners generally. You will need to rely on your own instincts and experience as you meet and work with individual landowners in your acquisitions.

WHO OWNS THE LAND AND WHAT EXACTLY DO THEY OWN?

One of the first things to look into during the early investigation of a property is who owns the land. You need to determine who you should talk to about the land and who can arrange for you to see it. Identify exactly what is owned and whether the ownership is complicated by reserved third-party rights, leases, easements, tax liens, mortgages, or other encumbrances that might impair title.

The Forgotten Co-Owner

The Upper Lake Land Trust finally had an opening to talk with the elderly Mrs. Thomason about her beloved Pine Shores Ranch property. Land trust staffer Helen Waits met with Mrs. Thomason seven times over a period of nine months, and her labors were rewarded by an agreement to purchase the property at a great discount from its full value. When the trust's attorney sent out a draft contract, Mrs. Thomason called Helen and told her that a copy should go to her sister in Alaska because her sister owns a one-fifth interest. Don't worry, said Mrs. Thomason, this won't hold things up. But Mrs. Thomason had not spoken with her sister in eleven years, during which time her sister had grown most avaricious. She wrote back to Helen a stark letter: "I will consider agreeing to this sale only when the price reflects the highest appraised value we can find." Helen sank. The deal was dead, or at least in need of complete restructuring. Nine months had been largely wasted. This could have been avoided, of course, had Mrs. Thomason been asked directly if there were co-owners, or if the land trust had obtained a title report showing complete ownership.

In the early stages of a project, it's best to find out as much as possible about ownership without investing too much money. Start by asking the landowner whether there are any others who have a legal interest in the property and whether he has a title report that can be shared. You can also ask for the deed by which the landowner acquired title.

Examine the property records in the county recorder's or assessor's offices. Be aware that recording documents about property can be complicated and recording systems vary by state and sometimes by county. Get a realtor or title company to help you do this research. In some states, realtors have access to computerized databases with information on property ownership. There are several ways to investigate title short of ordering a full title report (see Chapter 12, "Title").

LANDOWNER CONSTRAINTS AND MOTIVATIONS

There are many kinds of landowners and many reasons a landowner may be interested in working with your land trust. A landowner may want to protect family property or may be forced to sell because of financial difficulties. It is your job to be sensitive to these differences and to find a way to satisfy the landowner while achieving your own protection goals.

Here are motivations common to most landowners:

Economic return. Most landowners want to receive some economic return from their land. Not only can a land trust offer cash, it can offer tax benefits and enhanced value on adjacent land (which may also be owned by the landowner).

Timing. The timing of payments is frequently as important as the amount of payment. Landowners may need to sell quickly to raise immediate cash to send a child to school or pay emergency bills. A corporation may be interested in immediately ridding itself of a management headache. A land trust can move quickly without the bureaucratic constraints of a public agency or the financial and regulatory constraints of developers, which almost always cause them to insist on numerous contingencies (and therefore delays) in their deals.

Flexibility and creativity. Landowners often want to treat the disposition of their land in a very individual way, taking family members' desires into account and handling various portions of the property differently. Working with combinations of easements, reserved rights, and partial development, a land trust can design a project that meets the landowner's special needs while achieving its own conservation goals.

A Solution Only a Land Trust Could Provide

For years the Salmon River Trust had been trying to acquire a stretch of river highly susceptible to second home development. The key parcel, the Alton Camp, had been owned by the Altons since the 1930s. Mr. and Mrs. Alton, in their late seventies, decided they were no longer able stay on the property all summer, and they needed the money from sale of the property to fund their growing medical needs.

But they were not quite ready to give up for themselves—and their two children—the opportunity to come back each summer and sit on the stone porch by the river.

The trust found a solution—one most private buyers wouldn't offer and most government agencies couldn't offer. They would buy the property, giving the Altons a sizable down payment and quarterly installment payments for ten years. Moreover, the deed to the trust contained a reservation of rights that gave the Altons and their children (and their immediate families), during the lives of the Altons, the right to use the property for a total of two weeks every summer at times agreed by the family and trust. The trust would own, maintain, and use the property; the Altons could stay in contact with their special place on the Salmon.

Special Considerations for Entity-Owned Property

When the property in which you are interested is owned by, say, a corporation or a bank, your strategy and approach will be different than when working with an individual, but it will still be based on a process of identifying the owner's motivations and constraints.

Developers

Developers typically have straightforward goals. They want as much profit as possible and they want to free up capital to invest in additional projects. They also tend to be sensitive to local public opinion. Developers may be interested in working with a land trust that can bring credibility, support for necessary building permits and approvals, creative solutions to an impasse in the project, and, in some cases, tax benefits. (See "The Opportunities and Risks of Developer Easements," Joel S. Russell, *Exchange*, Winter 1993; the article focuses on easements, but many issues apply to purchases as well.)

Request the developer's sales literature. If the developer is a corporation, review its annual report. Talk to planning department staff or review their records to find out about the developer's past and pending development approvals. Talk to brokers and contractors who may have had business dealings with the developer. Find out who the developer's backers are, if any.

Be businesslike in your dealings with developers. Show them that you can offer them a deal that will work financially.

Be neutral in the public uproar that may surround the developer's project. Don't publicly collude with NIMBYs (people whose reaction to the proposed development is "not in my back yard") and advocacy groups opposing a project. Remain above the fray. Offer a solution to any public controversy along with a sufficiently attractive business deal.

Corporations

Corporations focus on increasing net returns to their shareholders. A corporation interested in selling its land is usually motivated by pragmatic considerations:

- The land is surplus, no longer serving a corporate interest.

- The land is a management headache or a financial drain (it neither produces an adequate return nor appreciates).

- The corporation needs to pay off a debt or get through a cash-flow pinch.

On the other hand, a corporation might be interested in a conservation sale either for the public relations benefits or for the tax benefits (they usually are well equipped to analyze and take advantage of these benefits).

Find out what you can about the corporation's current situation and probable direction. Read its annual reports and research it at the library. Most of all, however, find a way to talk to someone within the corporation about the corporation's interest in selling its land and about its decision-making structure.

Basic principles guiding corporate decision makers include:

- Avoid risk, such as legal action or questions raised by the IRS on an audit.

- Avoid public controversy.

- Get a commitment with no contingencies.

- Eliminate headaches that consume valuable executive energy.

- Eliminate waste and streamline the balance sheet.

- Produce net returns for the stockholders.

- Generate cash flow directly or indirectly (by reducing corporate taxes).

- Serve the broad public interest in the corporation's area of operation.

- Make deals quickly. (Delays increase costs.)

Following are a few simple guidelines for developing a successful proposal:

- **Do your homework.** Demonstrate professionalism by knowing the corporation, the land, your objective, and the numbers. Put it in writing.

- **Approach the corporation at the right level.** If the land is a significant asset and the corporation is small or mid-sized, it's worth locating a personal contact with the chairperson and pursuing an initial meeting with the chairperson or the key decision maker. Don't, however, besiege the chairperson on a minor matter.

- **Respect the hierarchy.** After you solidify your contact with the decision maker in an initial meeting, be prepared to touch base with the players at other levels.

- **Don't question motivations.** Second-guessing corporate objectives or philosophy will not help produce a transaction.

- **Avoid complexity in your proposal.** The corporate lawyers prefer a deal that is straightforward. Any complexity should be their complexity.

- **Provide precedent.** Most corporate executives want to follow a known path.

- **Establish your credentials.** Can you pay for the land? Which people in the corporate world will vouch for you? What's your track record (particularly with corporations)? What qualifies you to judge the value to the public of this project?

Estates

Those who manage estates (usually "trustees") always operate under the constraints of "fiduciary responsibility" to the estate beneficiaries. Their over-riding concern is providing the beneficiaries with the greatest financial return on the estate. Estates generally need simple, quick, all-cash deals at a price close to fair market value.

Find out who the decision maker is for the estate. This may be a trustee or the executor, who sometimes is the estate's attorney. (In any event, the estate's attorney usually plays a pivotal role in the decisions made by the estate.) Ask who has the authority to make decisions; review the relevant documents, agreements, and files in the probate court. Also, make sure someone on your team understands the probate process, which varies from state to state.

Banks/Distressed Properties

Properties are termed "distressed" when they must be sold because of the owner's financial difficulties. The entity authorized to handle the property will depend on the situation. If the property is subject to bankruptcy proceedings, the bankruptcy trustee will have authority. If it is a pre-foreclosure sale, the owner will retain authority; if it is a post-foreclosure sale, the lender's loan officer or real estate division head will have authority. But there are characteristics that hold true for most sales of distressed properties. Whether the sale is an auction or a foreclosure sale, those who sell the land are looking for a quick, all-cash, maximum-value sale. In most cases, there is little room for negotiation. In addition, the time you have to investigate a purchase of a distressed property is compressed since once your bid is accepted, you must buy or forfeit your deposit.

The rules relating to sales of distressed properties vary widely. Some entities authorized to handle distressed property, such as the Federal Deposit Insurance Corporation and Resolution Trust Corporation (which sell properties formerly owned by failed banks and savings-and-loans), can offer financing; others, such as banks handling loan foreclosures, cannot. You need to thoroughly understand the rules and procedures for the sale in question. Usually, you can simply call and request the rules.

Chapter 5

COMMUNITY SUPPORT

Community support is as essential for the success of a project as it is for the overall success of your land trust. It is a measure of the public value of a project and a source of help for the range of tasks that need to be done, including fundraising, gaining political approvals, and managing the technical aspects of the transaction. As many local people as possible must be personally vested in a project if it is to be successful. With enough community support almost every project can be done.

Presumably, your land trust works closely with community members as part of its overall, on-going protection program, and you have a good feel for the community's reaction to a specific project. Gauging this reaction early on will help you:

- identify the best, most practical long-term protection strategy

- identify sources of help and of opposition

- determine how to bring community elements together to promote the project

- stand on solid ground in your negotiations with a landowner (it can help you guess whether a landowner has a realistic alternative to conservation)

- identify ways to use your project to strengthen the finances and programs of your land trust

COMMON HURDLES

Community members may object to a project on a number of grounds.

Property tax loss. Property taxes are the lifeblood of local communities. If you plan to remove the property from the tax rolls, find out what the property taxes are and consider how much might be lost to the community. Compare (and prepare to defend) taxes that will be lost if the land is protected versus costs to the community of additional services if the land is developed. (See *Economic Benefits of Open Space*, Land Trust Alliance, 1994.) Prepare a case statement that explains the public value of the project.

Some land trusts simply decide it's best not to seek exemptions on land they own, or they arrange to make payments in lieu of taxes.

Seeking Property Tax Exemptions

As a nonprofit organization, a land trust frequently is exempt from property taxes on the property it holds (the basis for this exemption varies from jurisdiction to jurisdiction). If you expect to hold the land for any length of time and you will take over tax payments, you may want to file for property tax exemption. Before you do, investigate local and state policy on property tax exemptions and talk to neighboring land trusts or other nonprofits about how their applications for property tax exemptions have been treated.

When not to apply for tax relief. There are a few cases in which your land trust might not want to apply for a property tax exemption. These include:

- Your land trust is acquiring a piece of land that will not be used for conservation purposes. For example, if you have a donated piece of land that you expect to sell to raise money, you may not be able to obtain an exemption.

- Seeking an exemption might threaten your land trust's relationship with a community. (Some trusts seek exemptions but make payments in lieu of taxes.)

- Your land trust is holding a property for only a short time before passing it on to a public agency. In such instances, paying the taxes may be worth saving the time and trouble of filing for an exemption.

Stewardship plan poses a nuisance for neighbors. Among the most common objections to public use of land are noise, trespassing, increased crime or vagrancy, and increased traffic. Consider how stewardship activities on your land will affect neighbors. Prepare an analysis showing that these concerns are groundless or manageable.

Competing public uses. Others in a community may have their eyes on the property for public use other than as open space, for example as a site for a needed school. Some of these potential uses may be described in a general plan, but often you will learn about them by chance. Enlist your board members to always be looking for these kinds of conflicts. Pursue discussions early on with others proposing alternative uses for the land.

Competing private uses. Farmers, developers, loggers, or others may hope to use the land. While sometimes these offer you the "threat" around which to galvanize public support, often the public economy depends on such private initiatives. Be aware of who else might want the property, understand the alternative they would present for the community, and be prepared to explain your land trust's proposal. Better still, seek common ground: turn the competition into cooperation on a better alternative. Your land trust might be able to develop a lease agreement with a farmer, for example.

Steward objectionable to some members of community. You may determine that the most practical way to protect a property is to convey it to a public agency. Members of the community may oppose this, because they dislike either government in general or this particular agency. Have your board members put out feelers about your prospective plans for the property and find out what people will think.

Appearance that land trust is developer. As a "lesser of two evils" or for other legitimate reasons, you may propose a limited development as the best way to protect the critical portion of the land. Limited developments, while sometimes the only source of money to pay for important protection, can be controversial and stridently opposed by local residents. It can cost you credibility in the community if you are seen as just another developer. State clearly and often why the compromise was required and what benefits result.

Appearance of self-dealing. As a nonprofit, your trust should without question avoid all self-dealing, such as private gain by board members from land trust transactions. But there are times when, despite a clear public benefit to a transaction and compliance with the land trust's internal policy on conflict of interest, there is an appearance of self-dealing. Be rigorous in your documentation and as open as possible in your dealings. Your board must weigh the risk of seriously undermining public confidence.

Past investment in a project. Sometimes an individual or community group will have been involved in a project at some level—such as by opposing a general plan amendment or a subdivision approval—long before your land trust began working on it. These individuals or groups can be great allies, but they also can work against you if they feel they have been cut out of the deal or have not received the recognition they deserve.

WHO ARE THE COMMUNITY PLAYERS AND HOW CAN THEY HELP?

There are a number of people and groups in your community with whom you will want to maintain ongoing good relationships. In addition, each project particularly affects and involves a number of people. You will need to marshall the strength of supporters and to redirect those who oppose you. The key to this is understanding the various perspectives. For example, you may be interested in a property for its critical habitat; neighbors may be most interested in privacy; townspeople might see the land's development as a source of jobs and the protection effort as elitist. Your job is to find a way to appeal to every group's interest and focus support toward your goal.

Consider who would be directly affected—both positively and negatively. Who will be interested? Who should be interested?

Those you identify may play a variety of roles.

Adjacent landowners and neighbors. Your project may directly affect neighbors, particularly if there will be increased public use of the site. It's generally best to involve neighbors early on. Hold a public meeting to address their concerns about the property's future management and public access, and use their input to design the project so as to minimize its impact on them. (Whatever you do, some people may continue their NIMBY attitudes. If your project truly serves the overall public good, key decision makers should recognize this and support it despite some public criticism. If a lot of people object, however, you may have to accept that your project is unworkable.)

On the other hand, neighbors can provide excellent information about the land in the area and can help with contacts, fundraising, and political support. They may be willing to monitor the site when the project is completed and to lend their support to larger land trust goals.

Users of the land. It is always useful to know who, if anyone, uses or visits the land. A school district may offer field trips to the property, neighbors or other local residents may receive permission to cut wood or hunt there, and recreational users may hike or ski there, particularly if the property is adjacent to other recreation land and its boundaries are not well marked.

Also consider who the potential users of the land are; these may be your best supporters.

Major landowners. When embarking on a potentially controversial project, consider how landowners with similar property will react and how your chances of completing future projects with these landowners will be affected. In general, learn all you can about major landowners' backgrounds, interests, attitudes toward conservation, and political alliances. Look for connections to your board or to your supporters. Whether they are known to be supportive of or hostile to the land trust's goals, look for opportunities to meet them in an informal setting. Invite them to a land trust event, such as the celebration of a project closing or a fundraising activity. Ask a landowner you have worked with successfully in the past to go to an introductory meeting with the landowner of your new project.

Major donors. Major donors may provide influential contacts for your project and, of course, access to funding. Keep potential donors involved in land trust activities. Send them newsletters and include them in land trust events. Where appropriate, use their testimonials and contacts to approach landowners and potential new donors. If a donor is well known and respected in the community, you may even want to take her to an introductory meeting with a landowner. If a donor is politically well-connected, use him as a sounding board for a land protection project that may be controversial.

Community organizations. Consider other nonprofit organizations in the community, such as historical societies, church groups, garden clubs, scouting groups, block associations, service organizations (Kiwanis, Rotary, Lions, Elk, and Moose), bird-watching clubs, and fishing and hunting clubs. Review what you know about these organizations (their political and social clout, their relationships with each other). Consider reasons they might be particularly interested in this project and what useful skills their individual members might have. When groups are supportive, they may share their mailing lists with you, include articles about the project in their newsletters, and provide volunteers to help at fundraising functions, write letters, make phone calls, and appear at public hearings to lobby for public acquisition funds.

Any organized group can be a positive or negative force. Always consider what political baggage it brings to a project before deciding how you can work together. Although working toward a common goal, you may need to maintain your distance to be effective.

Realtors and land planning consultants. Explore possible cooperative arrangements with realtors and land planning consultants. Realtors can sometimes inform you of upcoming sales. Realtors and private planners also have useful information about trends in the real estate market and may be able to provide comparative sales information useful in your negotiations.

Developers. Consider local developers' attitudes toward your project. Sometimes developers who specialize in urban "in-fill" development may oppose development that sprawls into the greenbelt and onto existing farmland. Developers with these enlightened views may be a source of project support, either financially or through political contacts. But weigh carefully public perception of this kind of support.

Business associations. Don't overlook this important constituency for land conservation projects. Business people and chambers of commerce may support your project for business reasons; open space protection enhances communities, frequently benefiting the economy, particularly in tourist areas.

Consider how land preservation will affect local business activities. Make a presentation before the local chamber of commerce and service organizations about your project and the benefits of open space preservation. If possible, include a slide show of the project site and share glowing reports of public support for the project.

Bankers. Bankers may provide valuable contacts with landowners or political support. In addition, they are potential trustees of estate property. They may help arrange a loan, tell you about available land and trends in sales and financing, or help you work on foreclosed property.

Keep on the good side of your local bankers by putting at least some of your land trust's savings in their bank (unless this presents a financial hardship).

Elected officials. Local, state, or even federal elected officials are key supporters on almost any community project. They can initiate supporting resolutions or legislation and lobby other elected representatives to add their support.

This can be especially important, perhaps essential, when you are seeking public funds or approvals from a public agency.

Use your board members, major donors, and local advocacy groups, such as the Sierra Club and League of Women Voters, to get the inside story on your elected officials and their attitudes on open space issues (and on this project, if possible). Try to meet elected officials informally. (It's best if an influential board member or one of the official's major donors can introduce you.) Invite legislators to a public meeting about the project, to a fundraising event, or for a tour of the property. If circumstances dictate, invite them to a landowner meeting. A wealthy and powerful landowner might give you and your land trust more serious consideration after such an introduction.

Always remember to give due credit and public acknowledgment to public officials who help the land trust succeed in a land protection effort. If the trust makes that elected official look good to constituents, that positive experience will be remembered next time you need his support.

Public agencies. Identify all the government agencies involved in land use issues, including:

- planning commissions

- conservation commissions

- community development agencies

- natural resource and wildlife agencies

- soil and water conservation districts

- tax assessor

- quasi-public agencies, such as special citizen committees

Planning and other agency staff can be valuable allies. They can tell you a lot about the policies and politics of land use in your area and can alert you to impending land use changes on properties you care about—for example, telling you when plans have been submitted for subdivision approvals. When you are researching background information on the project before meeting with the landowner, local planning staff can tell you how it is currently zoned, what development is permitted, and what approvals would be required to increase the density. This will not only assist you in your negotiations with the landowner but will also enable you to give clear instructions to an appraiser so that you can quickly obtain a preliminary estimate of value.

Make sure the agency staff understand how your land trust operates and in what circumstances you can be most effective. If they are aware of what you can do, they may be more inclined to recommend to elected officials an open space alternative to a proposed development. They also may direct landowners to your land trust.

Tips for Going Public

Get a sense of what is really possible for the project before you go public with it. Avoid encouraging false expectations or stirring up unnecessary controversy.

Maintain confidentiality in your real estate negotiations. One of the trickiest elements of project management is learning to walk the fine line between keeping key community members involved and revealing too much before the deal is sealed. Nothing can sour a relationship quicker than a landowner reading about the great deal they have just made with the land trust in the local paper before anything has actually been signed.

WATCH FOR OPPORTUNITIES

Keep the long-term view in mind, watching for ways to leverage the contacts and positive feelings the project generates into future opportunities. While the frenzy of a project tends to keep you focused on immediate tasks, try to lift your eyes occasionally to see possibilities for new project leads, new landowners to approach, new contacts, new membership possibilities, or favorable publicity about your land trust as an achiever.

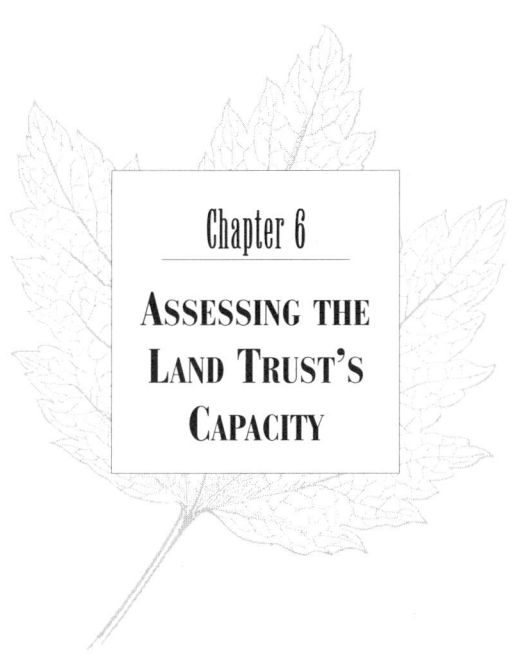

Chapter 6

ASSESSING THE LAND TRUST'S CAPACITY

There comes a point in your early research when you've gathered enough information to preliminarily consider the feasibility of the project for your land trust. It's time to look at your land trust's bottom line. Consider whether you have the resources it will take to complete the project and protect the land in the long term. Consider what could possibly go wrong and whether the land trust has the resilience to manage the project despite potential problems. In essence, you're looking at risk head on.

Projects demand an immense amount of energy from those involved. The myriad responsibilities of project management—building and maintaining relationships, meeting legal requirements, staying on top of deadlines, managing delays, keeping your board and your supporters informed—will be easier for you to handle if your land trust board is passionate about protecting the resource and you are personally committed to the job. This is particularly true when you are swamped with competing demands.

DO YOU HAVE THE RESOURCES TO COMPLETE THE PROJECT?

Evaluate Staff, Board Member, or Volunteer Capacity

It takes many people, with various contacts, skills, and professional expertise, to close a transaction. A project can fall flat if you do not have the people to handle all the tasks required within the time frame. Assess your land trust's "people" capacity by:

- identifying the major tasks in the project

- determining what skills, expertise, and time may be required

- identifying people on staff, on your board, or in your pool of volunteers (including experts willing to donate pro bono services) who are available

- considering what other priorities your land trust has, including other projects, and what will not get done if these people are involved in the proposed project

Evaluate Financial Capacity

Some projects at first appear (and indeed are) far too expensive for your land trust's land acquisition budget. But remember that there is more on the positive side of the equation than just the current bank balance—there are also the potentials for special fundraising, for a loan by a board member or bank, and for the involvement of an interested third-party buyer (conservation buyer, public agency, limited development).

Get a realistic idea of what the costs will be. (See Appendix C, "Project Costs Checklist.") Do at least a rough financial analysis of your cash flow over the life of the project and, ultimately, decide whether the protection strategy you envision (or any fall-back strategy) is feasible.

Your best guide in financial estimates is experience—your own or others. Talk to people who have completed projects. Ask about typical delays and surprise costs. Bring creative people together to brainstorm ways to fund your project. If your team does not include someone with strong financial skills, find someone!

OPPORTUNITIES AND RISKS

For every project you decide to pursue, you are at some level weighing the benefits against the risks. Grappling with the question of what is an acceptable risk can test the board's strength, and accepting risk requires a board that works hard, works together, and most of all has vision.

What Are the Opportunities?

A project can offer opportunities so compelling that your board is willing to assume a high level of risk.

A project may be something that your land trust simply has to do, even if it poses clear and daunting hurdles. The property may be the key parcel outlined in your long-range land protection effort. It may provide a critical buffer, which, if lost, would diminish the value of past acquisitions. It may offer you an exceptional opportunity for garnering public support and membership.

What Are the Risks?

Risks may be clear-cut and evident—such as an out-of-range price tag or predictable opposition by a vocal pro-development or NIMBY group—or they may require careful analysis to uncover. Ask yourself: What could possibly go wrong?

Financial loss. Your land trust could lose money on the project despite planning and precautions. A major donor might back out. Delays in subdivision approval for a limited development could mean unexpected interest payments. Agency funding could fall short at the last hour, leaving your land trust to make up the difference or lose credibility by dropping the project altogether.

Public controversy. Some projects, although they would clearly result in public benefit, may be controversial and may place the land trust in the midst of a public brawl. Think through the situation.

- How dependent is your project on public support?

- Will the land trust have a high or low public profile while doing the project?

- Is the opportunity for favorable publicity greater than that for bad publicity?

- Will key constituents be happy with the trust when the project is over?

- Will the ultimate use of the property prove controversial? Who will criticize the disposition, and how will this affect the land trust now or in the future?

- Are there any aspects of the trust's business dealings that might be perceived as unethical?

- How will your supporters respond to public criticism of the trust?

Failure to complete the project. A land trust that truly challenges itself to achieve its goals will probably not successfully complete every project it takes on. Always consider how your land trust's protection plan and public image would be affected if you fail to complete the project. Are you raising expectations irresponsibly? Balance your analysis with the recognition that failing to complete a project does not mean complete failure for your land trust.

DON'T GIVE UP!

Analyzing risk—and your land trust's capacity to manage it—highlights the project's strengths and weaknesses, helping your land trust narrow its choices for structuring the deal. Sometimes the risk seems so great your land trust will decide not to take the project on. Keep in mind that you have an alternative to dropping a project: cultivate it. Put the file away, but keep the project in the back of your mind. You might meet just the right person to help you; land values may dip; the opposition may be defused by a more compelling local issue. Time changes many features of a project.

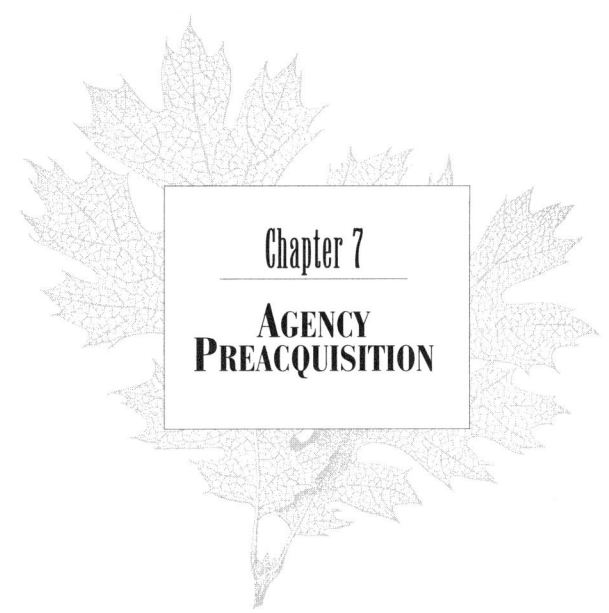

Chapter 7
AGENCY PREACQUISITION

P ublic conservation agencies are increasingly turning to land trusts for help in acquiring threatened properties. Land trusts' ability to act quickly in the private market and maintain flexible working relationships make them ideal partners in assisting and supporting public land acquisition programs. When public and land trust conservation priorities coincide, land trusts can "preacquire" land for public agencies by acquiring it from a landowner, then conveying it to the agency for conservation management for the public benefit. Through preacquisition, the conservation agency acquires land it might not have been able to obtain on its own, and the land trust helps to protect high priority land.

When a Preacquisition Makes Sense

A land trust should consider a preacquisition when the agency is unable to complete an acquisition on its own and one or more of the following factors are present:

- A property with conservation values lies adjacent to or within the boundaries of land owned and managed by a public conservation agency.

- A property is specifically targeted for acquisition by an agency for a new park or open space preserve.

- A property includes outstanding resources that an agency is specifically set up to protect.

- A property fulfills open space or other requirements for protection in a county general plan.

- The land trust can get a bargain on the property and pass the savings on to an agency that wants to own the property.

A preacquisition may be useful when your land trust does not have the financial resources to buy, hold, or manage land on a permanent basis, but can negotiate a deal that will satisfy the landowner's needs, the agency's requirements, and its own mission.

How the Land Trust Can Help an Agency

A land trust's role in a preacquisition largely involves adjusting or compensating for the variables—timing, price, land configuration, and special landowner circumstances (for example, a desire to have some continued use of the land after its sale)—to meet the needs of the acquiring agency.

Fewer timing constraints. A landowner may need to sell quickly to meet financial obligations or to close a transaction within a certain calendar year. Public agencies rarely have funds available for immediate acquisition and frequently have lengthy procedural and approval requirements. A land trust can step in and option or purchase land; it can structure a phased purchase for multiple parcels or schedule payments to fit the budget or timing of an acquiring agency.

Flexibility and creativity. Some agencies are forbidden by statute or regulation from holding, splitting, combining, and reselling parcels on the open market, all of which a land trust is free to do. When an agency, for example, needs or can afford only a portion of a parcel or when it needs to acquire multiple parcels from different owners to accomplish a single project, a land trust can step in.

Access to special funding. A land trust can:

- promote a bargain sale to bring the price of a project within an agency's budget

- generate donations from individuals, foundations, and corporations

- combine funds for an acquisition from a variety of public and private sources, such as agency funds, donations, or development mitigation funds

- generate funds through a partial development of the property if appropriate

Expertise and assistance. The land trust may provide the extra hands needed to complete a project as well as expertise in negotiations, tax incentives, and other legal matters.

Public support. Land trusts can help public agencies gain support for land projects that are agency priorities. One of the main benefits a land trust brings to an agency is the ability to garner public support for open space bond issues and acquisitions. While land trusts are prohibited from supporting or opposing political candidates, they can lobby for legislation, subject to expenditure limitations based on their overall expense budgets. They can inform and inspire local business groups, landowners, and neighborhood associations, garnering important votes and letters to legislators and public agencies. In fact, for many preacquisitions, this is a major part of the project manager's work.

Be careful, however, to avoid driving public agendas by optioning land that is not a high public priority, then lobbying for government purchase.

Independent stance. Some landowners prefer not to deal with public agencies. In these cases, land trusts can be valuable independent third-party negotiators. They can also step in when negotiations have collapsed, often defusing tension or breaking a deadlock. They also can help out when an agency faces statutory or procedural barriers to negotiation. It's a good idea to let the landowner know that you are negotiating the purchase for eventual public ownership. Land trusts can help assure good landowner and community relations by giving them a clear understanding of the ultimate use and disposition of the property.

Recovering Costs

As with any acquisition, a land trust undertaking a preacquisition project incurs a number of costs over and above the purchase price. It may also put its own financial resources at risk and forgo the opportunity to protect other important properties. It is reasonable for a land trust to expect to be compensated for these costs and uncertainties: if the agency acquired the property directly from the landowner, it would have to incur all the acquisition costs and uncertainties itself. The most common way for the land trust to recover these costs is to negotiate a bargain purchase (paying a price below fair market value) and then sell the property to the agency at or near fair market value. Sometimes a land trust, however, must pay fair market value for a property; in these cases, some agencies may be able to cover the land trust's costs over and above the purchase price.

However, there can be good reason for a land trust to cover its own costs or to pass on some or all of the savings from a bargain purchase to the agency. Sometimes a land trust will even transfer the property to the agency at no cost. This may make sense when the agency must use limited discretionary funds for a purchase, or during a period when the agency has little or no acquisition funds available to it. A land trust may lose money on some preacquisitions, and gain on others. The goal is to preserve important land resources, with each participant contributing the time, resources, and expertise it is best able to provide.

Be sure to understand in advance and respect agency policies regarding payment for preacquired properties and take care not to be overly aggressive.

Some Caveats

Preacquisitions are complex, and any land trust embarking on one should be aware of the following.

- An agency may have a great many steps and contingencies in its acquisition process. You can get pretty far down the road only to find that the agency will take much more time than you had projected to acquire the land, or even that it is prohibited from doing so.

- Agency projects can be subject to political whims and can be dropped when legislators or high-level agency managers move on.

- An agency's internal regulations governing the acquisition process can change midstream. These changes are particularly hard to anticipate when working with federal agencies, since a change in policy in one region may result in new regulations affecting all regions.

- Your land trust might get stuck holding land it is not prepared to manage if the agency funds don't come through.

Other Ways Agencies Work with Land Trusts

An agency may be able to:

- manage property for your land trust under a permit or lease agreement

- provide training and assistance through such programs as the National Park Service's Rivers, Trails, and Conservation Assistance Program

- offer technical assistance (appraisals, surveys, etc.)

- make outright grants to your land trust to acquire or manage land

---

GETTING TO KNOW PUBLIC AGENCIES

Working with the agency will always be easier if you have already established a personal relationship with agency staff. It will not only help you through a difficult project, but also open up new opportunities for joint projects and strengthen your land protection program overall. It takes time to cultivate these relationships, and you must take care in building them; one bad experience between your land trust and the agency can affect your relationship for years, even decades.

Establishing a Relationship with the Staff

If you're not sure which agencies in your area acquire land, review maps or talk to your community contacts, particularly those who have been involved with land protection campaigns. Ask agency staff to explain the agency's structure, acquisition priorities, and management philosophy.

But before you call for the first time, find out about your land trust's past relationship with the agency. Did anyone from your land trust meet with the agency in the past? When? Has your land trust ever worked on a project with the agency? Did any problems occur, such as friction between the personalities involved or failure on either side to carry out agreements? Has the agency had a bad experience with any other land trust? If so, what can be done to establish your credibility?

The people who staff and manage the agency will be your best sources of information and the links on which your relationship with the agency will depend. Take agency resource managers or acquisition staff out to lunch and find ways to maintain the contact. Build rapport and develop their trust—both in you and in your land trust—before you find yourself in the heat of a project crisis.

Keep in mind that agencies (particularly federal agencies) may have lots of staff in the loop: for example, district rangers, supervisors, and resource or hazardous waste specialists. Learn about the agency's staff structure and make sure you don't overlook a staff person who should be informed of your activities. (For example, if your agency contact is in a policy or planning position, be sure also to request a meeting with the land acquisition staff, since you will likely be working with them on a day-to-day basis.)

Agency staff are subject to a high degree of public scrutiny, and often must factor into their decisions how they will be perceived by their constituents, legislators, and the general public. Be considerate and carefully persistent.

Learn about the Agency's Acquisition Authority and Process

Public agencies vary widely in size, purpose, and administrative structure and operate within a complex system of constitutional, legislative, and judicial authority. Every agency that acquires land is constrained by the bounds of its authority and a rigorous acquisition process with various levels of required approvals, as well as legal and political impediments. You will need to find out exactly what it takes from project initiation to closing for the agency to buy land.

Legal authority. As a general matter, a governmental body—be it local, state, or federal—can acquire land only as authorized. The legal authority to acquire land and the authorization process vary from agency to agency and one locality to the next. Some agencies have broad powers, while others are severely limited or need special authorization for certain transactions. For example, a public agency may have the general authority to acquire land within the boundaries of park units, but require legislative authorization to acquire land outside the boundary.

Funding restrictions. The funding source may impose constraints or requirements. Bond issues may include language that details exactly what kind of land can be acquired with the bond monies, specifying, for example, that only a particular species' habitat or only "natural lands" (that is, without improvements) can be acquired.

Internal procedures. Agencies usually must follow specific internal procedures or policies for acquiring land, designed to assure that public money is spent appropriately. For example, almost all agencies require appraisals to confirm the value of land. On the other hand, an agency may have the legal authority to take certain action (such as acquire land through eminent domain), but may as a matter of policy not use this action. Local agencies are generally more flexible than federal agencies.

Applicable law. Agencies must comply with laws, such as applicable state or federal environmental impact report requirements and local land use laws. This may lengthen and complicate the process.

Questions to Ask an Agency

Authorization and Approvals

- Does the agency have the authorization to complete the project? Can it get authorization?

- What approvals are necessary to secure funding?

- What are the steps in this approval process? How do they relate to other time lines (such as state or federal budget cycle, commission or committee meetings, etc.)?

- Which agencies or individuals need to sign off on the acquisition?

- Who makes the final decision to acquire the land?

- Should the land trust make a presentation to a director or commission to ensure support for the acquisition?

Technical Requirements

- Which agency regulations apply to the acquisition?

- What are the steps in the agency acquisition process?

- What is required before the agency can sign a contract to acquire the land from the land trust? What contingencies will likely be in the contract?

- Must an appraisal be done? At what stage? How is the value approved? Must the appraiser be employed by the agency?

- Do the agency's title requirements and procedures differ from standard, private practice?

- What are the survey requirements?

- What state or federal laws apply, what are the requirements, and how will these affect the time line?

Funding Source/Requirements

- What is the source or potential source for funds: Legislative appropriation? Bond act? Operating budget? Dedicated fund (such as real estate transfer taxes, percentage of property taxes, lottery funds, license plate proceeds)?

- Does the agency have the funding in hand or will it have to get it from a legislative appropriation, issuance of a bond, or approval of funds from another unit of government?

- When will the funds be released?

- Are appropriations project-specific or are they general, allowing the agency to pursue projects at its discretion? If the latter, what is the agency's process for prioritizing?

- Once funds are approved, what are the steps to obligate them? What is the likely time frame before the agency can close on the acquisition?

- What special requirements may be placed on the project because of the source of funding (such as approval by the fund's administrative committee)?

- Is an exchange an acceptable possibility for the agency? Are exchange lands available?

Understand the Agency's Political Constraints

Because agencies' existence depends on public opinion and support, virtually all agencies are sensitive to changing politics. When elected administrations change, there may be changes in agency leadership. Be sensitive to changing priorities and consider how politics may be pressuring the agency.

Publicly give credit to agencies for their accomplishments. Your land trust will benefit from sharing the limelight.

RESEARCHING THE FEASIBILITY OF A PREACQUISITION

Researching preacquisitions can be difficult. Not only do you need to learn about all the steps and requirements in the agency's acquisition process, you also need to analyze intangibles: What is the agency's commitment to you and to the project? How credible are the time line predictions? What are the realistic chances, everything considered, of completing the project?

You need to ask the *right* people the *right* questions. Be sure you are talking to people who have access to complete and accurate information. Try to deal with higher-level people who can make decisions as well as provide the right information. You might enlist one of your trustees or an elected official interested in your land trust to help you reach the right people and perhaps to accompany you when you meet with agency personnel. Be sure you understand the information and haven't missed something important. It can be helpful, as a double check, to talk to additional agency staff or have others confirm what you have learned.

What Agencies May Have an Interest in the Project?

Consider all kinds of agencies whose priorities may overlap with yours, even those whose purposes may seem different from yours. For example, a water management district may have the authority to acquire land to protect groundwater resources—which could also protect scenic values, migratory bird habitat, or other resources. Numerous other agencies may be able to acquire land or easements, including flood control districts, agencies needing to provide mitigation land (such as those expanding ports or utilities), and agencies that need to acquire land to settle lawsuits.

Talk to your agency contacts or review the agency budget to find out how much is allocated to land acquisition. Is this allocation generally increasing or decreasing? Does the budget allocate specific amounts for specific projects? In times of budgetary constraints, there can be pressure to reshuffle funds within the agency. Ask your agency contact whether monies might be drawn down by other, higher priorities, including agency activities other than acquisition.

How Strong Is the Agency's Interest?

Once you've identified a potential project and an agency (or several) that may be interested in the land, determine the level of the agency's interest in completing the acquisition.

Is the project an agency priority? Ask whether the property or a portion of it is on the agency's priority list, fits within its long-range plan, or is otherwise of interest.

If a property is a low priority, don't push too hard. While your land trust may legitimately work to shape public open space policy, you can jeopardize a relationship with an agency if the agency feels pressured.

What has been the agency's history with the project? Ask how long the agency has been interested in the project. Find out what (if any) steps the agency has taken in the past to secure the land. Who on staff was involved in the project? Why was the project dropped or what slowed its progress?

Is the project being pushed by an individual, rather than by the agency? Sometimes a property may be an agency priority mainly because it is the pet project of an agency manager or a legislator from the district. If you suspect this is the case, be careful. You can find yourself involved with a project that is resented by agency staff or perceived as a pork-barrel project by the public. You can also wind up with a dropped project on your hands when the individual is promoted to a new area or is voted out of office.

Can the Agency Complete the Project?

Even if an agency wants to do a project, you need to make sure it has the resources to see it through.

What are the agency's current or potential sources of funding? Funding sources change over the years with elections and the changing economy; some sources of acquisition funds are obscure, and agency staff sometimes are unaware of them; funds that agency staff informed you were "unavailable" might suddenly appear at the agency's fiscal year end when portions remain unspent. Talk to as many people as possible, particularly influential people with contacts in the agency or the legislature.

What are the timing constraints on these funds (and how credible are predictions)? In most states, the availability of acquisition funds is tied to the agency's budget process. Funds for a specific acquisition or for an agency's acquisition program may be appropriated in one fiscal year, but they may not be available for spending until the start of the next fiscal year. At the federal level, projects and expenditures generally require special approval by congressional committees, a process that is tied to the federal budget process and is highly uncertain.

It's important to reassure yourself that the time line projected by agency staff is realistic. Put your understanding of it in writing for your agency contact to verify, and confirm it with other knowledgeable contacts.

What is the agency staff's capacity and experience? Make sure there will be agency staff available to finish the project in the time frame established by the funding source and ask how many and what kinds of acquisitions the staff has completed. If you foresee a specific problem with the project, such as a tricky appraisal issue, find out whether the agency knows how to handle it.

Managing a Preacquisition

A preacquisition involves two real estate deals, one with the landowner and one with the agency. You are in the middle, but you can take precautions to manage your risks. First, negotiate an option to purchase (see Chapter 8, "Finalizing Your Plan"), preferably one with a long enough term that you don't have to commit to the acquisition until the sale to the agency is assured. Ideally, you can acquire the property and immediately convey it to the agency, in a so-called "back-to-back" closing that dramatically reduces your risk. Second, work to assure agency's timely purchase by building community support, adhering strictly to the agency's requirements and process, and nudging the bureaucratic process.

Throughout the process, try to meet directly with the key individuals and bodies that have veto and approval power. Unless you reach the proper understandings at those levels, you can be derailed at any time. Keep in mind that the key decision maker may not be the titular head of the agency. An agency director, for example, may be occupied with policy matters or external meetings, leaving the hands-on project work to staff.

Preacquisitions rarely are easy and are notorious for their delays. The agencies' procedural requirements (public notice, appraisal review, environmental impact statements, and so forth) and the funding approval process generally prohibit quick action.

Know and Follow Technical Requirements

To work comfortably with an agency, you should understand and follow all of the steps in the acquisition process, paying particular attention to their timing.

Risks of Interim Acquisition

If your option expires before you are able to close with the agency or if you simply are unable to negotiate an option at all, your land trust can acquire and own the land for an interim period before conveying to the agency. But you must carefully weigh the risks.

Removes incentive. Once your land trust has purchased and secured a property, the immediate threat disappears. This may diminish the agency's incentive to secure funding and delay closing. The worst-case scenario is that acquisition funding does not come through and your land trust is left holding property it can't afford.

Ties up limited funds. Acquiring the land makes your own funds unavailable for other projects.

Increases project costs. If you acquire property, you will add financing costs (interest, staff time seeking financing), acquisition costs (title insurance, recording fees), and holding costs (property taxes, insurance, maintenance) to your overall transaction costs.

Increases your liability. Owning land for even a short while brings liabilities and management responsibilities.

Increases potential for loss. Land may lose value due to zoning changes or market fluctuations. It is particularly risky to acquire property in a deteriorating market or when the value of land or its natural resources (coal, timber, etc.) may be temporarily inflated by speculative conditions. Of course, property may also increase in value, but you should not count on this in planning your project.

Sit down with key players before the project gets too far along and make sure that everyone shares a common objective and agrees on procedures, decision points, and so forth. (These understandings can be broad. For example, some land trusts that work frequently with a particular agency develop a blanket memo of understanding with the agency.) Ask if the agency has anything in writing describing the process, including the rights of those selling to the agency.

Pay particular attention to the following technical requirements.

Appraisal requirements. Generally, an appraisal needs to be done for any preacquisition. (See Chapter 15, "Appraisals.") Regardless of who completes the appraisal—the agency or the land trust—the agency's review appraiser must approve it.

Begin by deciding whether the agency or land trust will handle the appraisal. Most of the time, things will run more smoothly if the land trust manages the appraisal process. If you are handling it, the following tips are important:

• Stay in close communication with the agency through the appraisal process.

- Make sure you understand all the agency requirements for the appraisal, including what limiting conditions they will accept and any special standards that should be shared with the appraiser.

- Select an appraiser whose work the agency respects and whose qualifications the agency will accept (and ask whether the agency keeps a list of recommended appraisers).

- If you use someone who is not on the agency's list, be sure your appraiser understands the concerns of the agency's review appraiser. Organize a conference before the appraisal work begins to allow your appraiser and the review appraiser to discuss potential issues.

- Review the completed appraisal and suggest relevant adjustments prior to forwarding it to the agency for review.

Title. Both the land trust and the agency must approve title. Agencies' title requirements vary. Early in the project, initiate a title search to identify issues that might affect the agency's acquisition. These include deed restrictions, reservations of use, and encumbrances. (Many agencies cannot accept deed-restricted land.) Once the title report is complete, have your attorney review it and analyze the impact of any title exceptions. After this, send it to the agency for its approval.

Pin Down the Agency's Commitment

To bring a preacquisition to a successful close you need to press for commitments. In part, this involves focusing public support for the land's protection, and putting the project in the forefront with the agency and with your legislators. But there are several levels of commitment you can seek from an agency that will help secure your deal.

Assurance of availability of funds. Unless the agency already has funds it will designate for the land under consideration, the first step is to get the acquisition funds committed to the project, typically through an appropriations bill or bond measure. Explore whether the language of the appropriations bill or bond measure can limit the use of funds to buying the property you will preacquire. The more specific this language is, the greater the assurance that the funds will be spent on the project you are undertaking.

Suppose, for example, that your land trust is preacquiring a property from the Gaines family on the Wolf River in the Black Rock State Forest with the expectation of conveying the property to the forestry division of the state Division of Natural Resources for $200,000. The language of the appropriations bill might be as general as "$5 million to the Division of Natural Resources for open space acquisition" or as specific as "$5 million to be expended as follows: $200,000 for the Gaines Tract on the Wolf River in Black Rock State Forest...." Obviously, you will want to do what you can to get specific language.

Letters of intent. Letters of intent define the land trust/agency relationship and outline the acquisition procedure, time line, method and amount of reim-

---

Warning: Agency Funds Can Vanish!

Even if the acquisition funds are earmarked specifically for the property you are preacquiring, they can disappear in a variety of ways:

- the legislature rescinds the funding

- the actual sale of bonds may be subject to an appropriations decision by elected officials or to the discretion of the agency

- funds, if not used, may evaporate at the end of the fiscal year (and what constitutes "used" is often confusing)

- bond sales may be postponed if a decline in interest rates is anticipated

- small bond sales may be packaged with others and brought to market only two or three times a year

- a government may be subject to a monthly debt ceiling, and if emergency road repairs are needed, your "discretionary" project may be delayed

If your land trust does rely on broadly discretionary funding, identify who has this discretion and get a full explanation of the process by which this discretion is exercised.

---

bursement of the acquisition costs, and so forth. They generally are not enforceable, but they do provide a clear indication of the agency's intent to acquire the property. You should be aware that, depending on the laws and policies governing the agency you are working with, the Letter of Intent may be public information. If so, you will want to be sure the landowner understands that. (Chapter 8, "Finalizing Your Plan," covers letters of intent more generally.)

Signed contract. The next level of security in a preacquisition is signing a contract. This may be in the form of an option (giving the agency the right—but not the obligation—to purchase the property), which will set the terms of the deal, or it may be in the form of a purchase-and-sale agreement. A signed purchase-and-sale agreement (or a notice that the agency has exercised its option) will usually obligate agency funds, that is, prohibit the funds being reprogrammed for another use. Most such agreements will include conditions (title meets agency standards, no contamination, subject to approvals) that provide an out for the agency.

Disbursement of funds. In a final stage of commitment, the agency can obligate funds by either depositing funds in escrow or writing a check to your land trust. Once you've reached this point, your land trust and your agency partner have succeeded in negotiating the often-hazardous maze of getting funds absolutely committed to the project you have been working to protect. Generally, provided the land trust can meet the terms of the escrow or otherwise close as required by the contract, the deal is done.

Section II

STRATEGY AND NEGOTIATIONS

As you progress in a project, you move into a phase of finalizing your plan (to the extent plans ever are final). You will want to move as quickly as possible to gain site control (that is, to make an agreement with the landowner that at least temporarily prevents sale of the property to anyone else) and to pin down your source of funds. Negotiating an agreement with the landowner that offers your land trust site control, adequate legal safeguards, and enough time to secure funding is the heart of doing projects. Once the deal is signed, what remains are the technical requirements of closing.

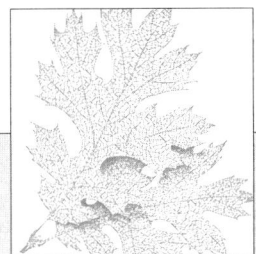

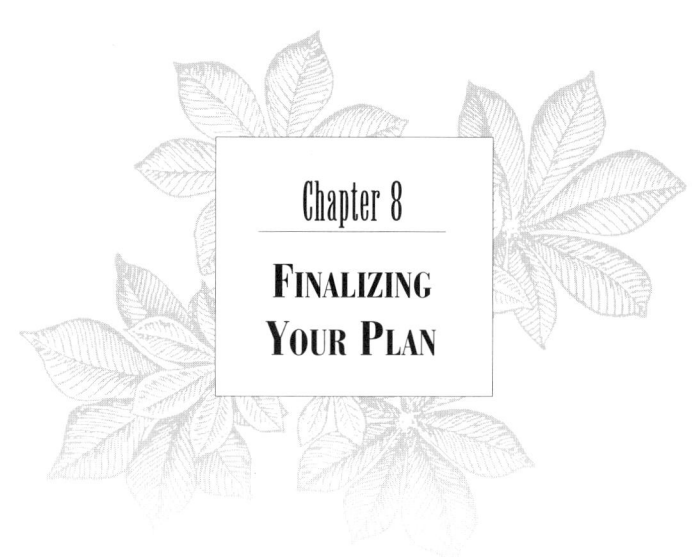

Chapter 8

FINALIZING YOUR PLAN

A t a certain point in the project, you will have a specific protection goal for the property, a good idea of where your money will come from, and enough information in hand to know what the technical issues are. Now is the time to lay out your action plan, thinking backwards from your protection goal to identify all the steps you need to take. Typically, these will include:

- acquisition steps (option, appraisal, title report, closing, etc.)

- financing arrangements (due dates, etc.)

- fundraising activities (meetings with key supporters, grant deadlines, mailings, etc.)

- political endorsements or approvals (meetings with officials and legislators, approval points, etc.)

- preparation for stewardship (baseline data collection, management plan, etc.)

A key intermediate objective in any acquisition plan should be to acquire "site control": the legally binding right for your land trust to acquire the land on terms established in a legal agreement. Site control gives you the kind of certainty you need—particularly certainty of price—to negotiate financing or mount a fundraising campaign. It pins down some parts of your project, around which you can finalize your action plan.

ACQUISITION AGREEMENTS THAT OFFER SITE CONTROL

There are a variety of forms of site control agreements. The most secure is an acquisition agreement that specifies the full range of circumstances that will govern the transfer of the property. By nailing down the details of the sale, you protect your land trust from uncertainties and buy time to research and analyze potential problems.

Purchase-and-Sale Agreement

A purchase-and-sale contract is the most common acquisition agreement used for the sale of real estate. The contract obligates the seller to sell and the buyer to buy, subject to specified conditions, and specifies basic terms, such as the time frame for closing, price, legal description of the property, and required condition of title. Once the contract is signed and the consideration (usually money) changes hands, the parties are *bound* to perform the contract. The conditions written into purchase-and-sale agreements typically offer "outs" for both buyer and seller. Clearly, it's in your land trust's interest to bind the seller, but because the contract binds both parties, you need to thoroughly assess the risks for your land trust if you don't perform, including loss of deposit and liability for damages.

Get Your Agreement in Writing

The Mesa Grande Land Trust reached agreement with the Moreno family to acquire their 200-acre ranch on the great mesa. They all shook hands and the land trust went to work finding funding.

They approached two local foundations, both banks in town, and several leading citizens, and they got a curious response. Funders seemed interested, but somehow reserved. It was a banker who explained the problem: If you are to be taken seriously, and people are going to go out on a limb to raise funds, you need a firm agreement to sell the property, one old man Moreno won't walk away from.

The trust got the message. They had their lawyer draw up a purchase option contract, and it was presented to the Moreno family. It was not easy, but after a month they had a written agreement. Suddenly, they were taken seriously; they had site control and could deliver, and fundraising became easier.

Option

An option is essentially a purchase-and-sale agreement under which the owner of the land gives the other party, in exchange for some form of consideration, the *right* (but not the *obligation*) to buy the land within a certain period of time. Before the option expires, the buyer must either exercise his right and follow through on the terms specified in the document, or drop the option, in which case the seller is free to market and sell the property to another. An option binds only the seller, not the buyer. Usually, options involve the exclusive right to buy the land (multiple, nonexclusive options are sometimes sold, in which case the option holder that first exercises its option is entitled to buy the property).

An option provides the option holder time to consider the merits of the project and to put together a feasible deal. If you cannot make the deal work, you lose only the original option consideration.

Option consideration can be as low as $10, though some attorneys recommend a minimum of $100. Like a deposit, option consideration usually is credited to the purchase price. Typically, if the option is not exercised, the consideration is nonrefundable.

An option payment can also be structured as a loan. Structuring the option payment as a loan enables you to put down substantial money that will satisfy the landowner but not put you at risk. Instead of a nonrefundable option consideration, your loan is the consideration. Such a loan can even bear interest.

Because an option specifies all the terms of the acquisition, you should be as careful negotiating and considering the terms of the option as you would be with any other purchase-and-sale contract. In fact, one way to structure your option contract is to attach a standard purchase-and-sale contract to a cover letter that outlines the terms of the option, including consideration to be paid and time frames for exercising and closing.

Earnest Money Contracts

An earnest money contract (as it is called in the West and some other areas) is a variation of a purchase-and-sale agreement. Earnest money is a deposit made by a buyer of real estate (typically of a house) as a sign of good faith. Usually, this deposit is given at the time the sales contract is signed. It is then held in a separate account by a broker or escrow company until the sale actually closes. At that time, the earnest money is credited toward the purchase price. If, however, the buyer fails to complete the purchase (and has no legal excuse), the earnest money is forfeited to the seller as "liquidated damages" for the buyer's default. The seller is then free to make other arrangements to sell her property.

Earnest money contracts are often confused with options since the buyer will forfeit an agreed upon sum of money to the seller if he does not go through with the deal. An earnest money contract, however, is a contract to buy the property. If the buyer does not go through with the deal, he not only loses the earnest money, but also may be technically defaulting on the contract.

Donation Agreement

A donation agreement formalizes the transfer of donated property. This protects your land trust from the possibility of investing time and money in analyzing a gift only to have the gift rescinded. Just as with a purchase-and-sale or option agreement, you negotiate such things as condition of title, division of responsibilities with regard to contamination, and the timing of closing. The agreement can give the land trust the right to not accept the donation if the property is found to be unacceptable. It is businesslike and helpful for your land trust's planning to secure a donation agreement whenever any gift of land is offered.

The terms of a donation agreement may specify that the agreement is legally binding. The enforceability of donation agreements, however, varies state by state. Having a donation agreement will enhance, but not necessarily guarantee, enforceability.

Site Influence: Better than Nothing

Your land trust may not be able to negotiate or afford outright site control. There are many arrangements short of formal site control that are good halfway measures and can position you to gain site control later. These may cost little or nothing, while giving you time to research the project, marshall support, or simply get to know the landowner better. They also may be the best you can get.

Site influence agreements range from formal to informal. The more informal the agreement, the easier it is to get, particularly if it doesn't require attorneys. The agreements depend, however, on the continuing goodwill of the landowner.

Letter of Intent

Letters of intent anticipate future relationships and often are used to document an agreement, whether expressing the parties' intention to enter into a fully drafted acquisition agreement or detailing the understanding of how the property will be managed. These letters can range from a highly informal "napkin" agreement reached at a lunch meeting to a fairly detailed, countersigned letter that may meet the test of being a fully enforceable contract. They are typically used when you are unsure about a deal. If you are sure, you should seek an option or purchase-and-sale agreement.

Written letters of intent are useful for narrowing issues and identifying areas of agreement. They are risky, however, because they do not outline all the terms of the acquisition, yet they can be construed as a binding contract. (Law books are replete with cases evaluating the enforceability of letters of intent.) For any letter of intent that you sign, make sure that you include language stating that the parties will be bound only through a subsequent "fully drafted agreement." In addition, be sure your attorney reviews the letter.

Right of First Refusal

In a right of first refusal, the landowner agrees to inform you of her intention to sell to another party, giving you a chance to match the best offer, but you are not bound to buy. The problem is that you never know when, if ever, you can acquire the property. Furthermore, rights of first refusal typically require that your trust meet not only the price but also the terms of the best offer. If the competing offer is one that will close quickly, you may not be able to get your funding in place quickly enough to take advantage of your right.

Always record rights of first refusal in order to put other buyers on notice. Since buyers almost always review title records before buying a property and will not want to proceed unless the right of first refusal is honored, recording your right of first refusal will reduce the chances of your rights not being observed.

In addition, be sure that a third party offer is serious before matching it.

Lease

Leases typically give a land trust exclusive use or access rights to a property for a set time period. With a lease, you often can protect lots of land value by controlling land use with relatively little money; on the other hand, you do not receive all the benefits, while you might incur many of the liabilities, of land ownership. Leases give you a trial period to manage the property (you may determine that it's not workable for your trust), can be a terrific way to build public support if your lease allows you to bring the public onto the property, and allow you time to build your relationship with the landowner. In fact, you may determine that a long-term lease will work well as your protection goal. Leases vary widely in the degree to which they shift responsibilities of management and are subject to considerable negotiation.

A "lease-option" agreement is extremely useful. This allows your land trust to lease a property and, if you want, to purchase the land at the end of the lease (or during the lease term, if the lease so provides). Typically, some or all of the lease payments can be applied to the purchase price.

Wills and Bequests

If the landowner puts the land trust in his will, you will have complete control of the land on the owner's death. Until that time, however, the landowner is free to change his will. In addition, the timing of your control of the land is extremely unpredictable.

Management Agreement

A management agreement is less formal than a lease. It specifies a plan under which the property will be managed, either by the landowner (with the advice or assistance of the land trust) or by the land trust itself. These usually are recorded and remain in force for their full term even if the land changes hands. This kind of agreement provides no permanent protection.

Registration Program

Some land trusts operate programs to "register" significant conservation properties. This registration involves drafting a nonbinding agreement stating that the landowner will not develop the land, or at least certain portions of it, and will notify the trust of any threat to the land or plans to sell. The land trust provides advice on managing the resources and may visit the property annually to ensure these are being protected.

DEVELOPING AN ACTION PLAN

An action plan is essential for keeping a project's time lines coordinated. If your protection goal is outright fee acquisition of the land funded by a community fundraising effort, you might decide that your fundraising campaign can't be kicked off effectively until you've signed an option with the landowner. Before the option can be signed, you will need to develop a better understanding of the property's value. Simultaneously, you may begin work on a media campaign publicizing the threat to the property as groundwork for your fundraising campaign. A careful plan won't guarantee you success but it will make it easier for you to keep things on track.

Typical Project Delays

- Fundraising target not met on time

- Grant application denied

- Bank does not approve loan

- Structures on land present liability problem

- Additional funds needed for maintenance

- Problem securing liability insurance

- Acquisition agreement takes longer to negotiate than expected

- Appraiser late with report

- Appraised value necessitates renegotiation of option contract

- Unexpected title defects need to be resolved

- With private sales, market is slower than expected

- Survey uncovers problem (encroachment, sovereign land, jurisdictional issue for preacquisition)

- Survey delayed until snow melts

- Environmental contamination discovered

- Agency review appraiser identifies problems

- Appropriation of funds for public agency purchase not available until following fiscal year

- Agency delays processing acquisition

Work with your team members to develop your plan, brainstorming alternatives and considering worst-case possibilities. Develop contingency plans for times when things don't go according to plan. Call upon experts to double-check your budget and time lines. (See Appendix B, "Project Tasks Checklist.")

- **Look at the big picture.** What are your major constraints? What is the overall time frame available? What resources are available?

- **Set milestones.** Set milestones such as ordering the title report and paying the option consideration. By scanning project milestones you quickly get a feel for the timing of project phases and of the project as a whole.

- **Identify and order tasks.** Decide what tasks must be accomplished to reach each milestone and in what order they must be completed.

- **Develop a realistic time line.** Unanticipated delays can kill your project. Keep your resources—time, money, people—in mind as you develop a project time line. Be realistic. Take all your projects into account and cross-reference your tasks. Be sure you're not trying to accomplish three months' work in one.

- **Monitor and track progress.** A plan should be used, not filed away! Update the time line as necessary. Keep your team members and project supporters apprised of changes.

We Just Need a Few More Weeks

The Herndon Development Corporation and the Red River Trust at last came to an agreement in which the corporation gave the trust a six-month option expiring June 30 (for $1,000) to purchase a critical stretch of wetland and upland hammock. The trust was sure they could raise commitments for the $130,000 purchase price from their donors and a nearby private college.

By mid-June the trust had commitments for $75,000 and "soft" assurances for $30,000 more, but the trust's board felt uneasy about exercising the option to purchase without all financing in place. They decided to ask the corporation for a 30-day extension of the option deadline. They discovered that things had changed, however. The corporation's former president had been fired, and the new executive officer faced a financially struggling enterprise. The new president declined to extend the option, convinced he could sell the property on the market for $200,000 under current conditions.

The trust was in a box. If they exercised, and failed to close due to a shortage of funds, they most certainly would be sued for damages. If they chose not to exercise the option, they would walk away from the option money and months of work. They chose to abandon the project. They learned that they should have negotiated for a year from the outset.

Purchase-and-Sale Timetable

	Landowner	Land Trust	County	Bank
March	Meet landowner, walk property; get rough value estimate from realtor.	Brief board on project, ask for their help.	Meet with open space agency staff; tour property; organize grassroots support for open space bond act.	Meet with local bankers for six-month loan to land trust until county can buy property.
April	Take landowner to other land trust sites; continue discussion; firm up estimate values.	Have board tour site, meet landowner.	Meet individually with county supervisors; tour site.	Get commitment for financing.
May	Send landowner non-binding offer letter; meet to discuss.		Conduct bond act letter writing campaign.	
June	Bring in attorney; draft and send out option agreement expiring in October; get it signed.	Order appraisal.	Bond act on ballot; voter approval; hearing on land acquisition.	
July		Review title and appraisal; complete environmental assessment.	Provide county with title report and appraisal; board of supervisors authorization.	Provide bank with title, environmental and appraisal information.
August	Give response to landowner and attorney on title and environmental assessment.	Obtain board authorization to acquire and sell.	Negotiate contract of sale with county; confirm title and environmental assessment; county approves appraisal.	Review and finalize loan documents with attorney.
September	Resolve title and environmental issues, if any.		Contract signed; county to purchase in March.	
October				

	Landowner	Land Trust	County	Bank
November	Exercise option; prepare for closing in 30 days.	File property tax abatement; prepare management plan; obtain insurance.	Open space bonds sold.	Fund loan at closing.
December	Close on and acquire property.	Hold and manage property.		
January				
February				
March		Celebrate, thank supporters, and coordinate press.	Complete sale to county.	Pay off loan; publicize and thank bank.

Developing Your Budget

The more complex your project, the harder it is to estimate your costs and the more pessimistic your budget should be. Build ranges into your budget figures or consider adding a contingency factor of 10 or 20 percent to allow for unforeseen cost overruns. These can include higher than expected sales price, appraisal fees, title fees, interest costs, staff costs, professional fees, and environmental assessments. (See Appendix C, "Project Costs Checklist.")

Estimate your income and develop a rough cash-flow chart for the project's anticipated life cycle, showing the timing of expenses and receipts, to ensure that expenses will always be matched by available cash. Consider alternative purchase strategies that minimize or eliminate cash-flow crises. And, as with all your project considerations, update the budget periodically.

The following questions can help you analyze the financial impact of your project:

- How much cash are you likely to invest in the project?

- Where will the money come from? If from your land trust's acquisition fund, what proportion is this of your overall budget?

- What are the timing requirements of cash outlays? During the course of the project, will there be major cash flow imbalances?

- Can the flow of payments to the seller be structured over a long period? Can payments be made refundable?

- What alternatives exist to making significant cash outlays?

- If things go wrong—the worst case—what is the maximum cash liability?

How Should You Plan?

There is no "right" way to develop a project plan. Project managers use all kinds of techniques, from long lists to sophisticated computer software. Find a planning method that works for you; a system you will use makes the difference between managing a project and managing a series of crises.

On pages 60 and 61 there is an example of a project time line. It assumes that you've already determined that the county would like to buy the property for a county park and that the open space bond measure to be voted on in the upcoming election is a likely source for the funds. It also assumes certain constraints: the landowner will not extend the option past October and agency purchase funds for this project will not be available until the following March (and possibly not at all if the bond measure fails). These facts set the basic parameters. The land trust will need to devote time and effort on the bond measure campaign and it will have to come up with interim financing.

GIVE YOURSELF LATITUDE

A project's risks generally are proportionate to its complexity. The more parties you need to satisfy, the more critical the technical issues, the higher the financial stakes—the more pressure you will be under. Building leeway into your project's time line and budget and developing fall-back strategies gives you the latitude you need to maneuver. This latitude is a key thing you negotiate in your acquisition agreement.

Chapter 9

PRELIMINARY NEGOTIATIONS: REACHING COMMON GROUND

Negotiating with the landowner is the most sensitive and critical step in any acquisition. Everything you learn in the earliest phases of your project—about the land and the landowner—is drawn upon and synthesized as you develop your negotiation strategy. Every contact you have with a landowner is part of your negotiations.

While no negotiation looks exactly like another (as no landowner or piece of land is exactly like another), there are certain basic phases in the negotiation process.

Getting the landowner on your side. Developing personal rapport and mutual understanding with the landowner is the critical first goal in your negotiations and the foundation for all your later agreements. It begins with your earliest meetings. Until you have developed this relationship, it makes little sense to move forward with other aspects of your deal.

Framing the deal. In the next phase of negotiations, you and the landowner uncover the issues and narrow areas of agreement and disagreement. This is the heart of your negotiations: If you can reach agreement on a basic framework for the deal, you will probably have 90 percent of your contract worked out.

Negotiating the specifics of the acquisition agreement. Once you've reached conceptual agreement, you formalize this in a contract. In most cases, you begin at this stage to work with an attorney as you draft your agreement with the landowner.

Renegotiating the deal. Rarely do deals close exactly as anticipated. There will almost always be continuing rounds of negotiation. Perhaps, in drafting the agreement, you encounter a title problem that cannot be resolved without an extension of your option period, which must be renegotiated. External circumstances might change the parameters of your negotiation. Or the landowner may have difficulty getting out of some prior obligation, such as a lease, and may request an extension of the closing date. Remain patient and flexible: Finalizing the agreement can take a long time.

Setting the Stage

Initiating Contact

There are many ways you can initiate contact, from a cold phone call to a simple introductory letter followed by a call, to a personal introduction by a board member at a social occasion. The method you choose will depend on the landowner, the circumstances, your land trust's preferred practice, and your own personal style. However you initiate contact, you should suggest a meeting to more fully explain what your land trust is and does.

Be cautious in presenting your land trust through written materials before you know something about the landowner's likes and dislikes. While it is a good idea to compile a presentation package that includes photos, maps, and other materials, these could strike the landowner as intrusive or presumptuous and leave a poor first impression.

Finding Out Who Is in Charge

Always try to meet directly with the legal owner of the land. Sometimes, however, you may find that you can't. You may deal with the adult child of a landowner who is failing in health, the attorney for a wealthy recluse, a realtor, or the land sales representative of a corporation. As early in the process as possible, find out who all the parties are that you may need to talk to. In addition to confirming who the legal owner is, you need to determine who has the legal authority to make a commitment and sign an agreement, who will participate in the negotiations, and who may be influencing the owner or the owner's representative behind the scenes.

There's no formula for answering these questions. You may have to do some detective work, and can find yourself treading in extremely sensitive areas. Be discrete and use good judgment. Sometimes only your intuition will tell you that you need to find out more about the parties. If you suspect there may be others you should be dealing with, it's probably wise to double-check.

Legal authority. If the owner of a property is an individual, he has the legal authority to sell the land. If the owner is a corporation, partnership, trust, estate, or other entity, someone within the organization may be authorized to approve a sale on the organization's behalf—and this may not be the person with whom you first begin discussions. Finding out who has this authority may be as simple as asking. It also may touch a sensitive nerve with the person with whom you have initial contact. If you're not sure, inquire delicately whether the negotiator has appropriate authority or whether there are others to whom you should talk. Ask this same question of others involved with the deal, such as the attorney, the broker, or the heirs, to corroborate what you are told.

Authorized representative. Sometimes the person you negotiate with represents the legal owner, just as you represent your land trust. While the representative may not have legal authority, this person may wield considerable control over the decision. How much control she has is something you can only learn through reliable sources, or by relying on your hunches. (When working with representatives, consider sending copies of documents to the legal owner.)

Behind-the-scenes decision makers. All matters of legal authority aside, people can be heavily influenced by those close to them. A spouse, favorite child, or close professional advisor may wield influence that can make or break a deal.

Getting to Know the Landowner

The primary objective of the first meetings with the landowner is to build personal rapport. You want to put the landowner at ease and talk on his terms about the land. You might engage in small talk, ask questions, admire the property and ask to be shown the landowner's favorite portions of it, eat and drink what's offered. Most of all, don't be in a hurry (unless the landowner clearly wants you to hurry). Find excuses to have repeated contact.

Asking questions can be a great way to learn not only about the land but about the personality and circumstances of the landowner:

- How long have you owned the property?

- How long has the land been in your family?

- What is the history of the land? How has it been used?

- What would you like to see happen to your property?

As a rule of thumb, keep business specifics out of the first meeting. You want to establish your personal relationship before you get into business. If the landowner turns to business, do what you can to postpone the discussion (but don't waste the landowner's time).

People almost always are sensitive about their personal financial matters. You probably shouldn't even bring the subject up in the first meeting. If it does come up, exercise caution and judgment. Often, you can learn a great deal about a landowner's financial situation indirectly from the conversation or independently from other sources. Be sure not to discuss the landowner's finances with the press.

Confidentiality is frequently a major concern for a landowner and a major selling point for your land trust. Reassure the landowner by asking, "Is this something you would like me to keep confidential?" Remind others involved with the project that confidential information must remain so. Keep anyone who is likely to be loose-lipped out of the circle.

Distinguishing Your Land Trust from Other Buyers

Right from the start, distinguish your land trust from other private-market buyers. The land trust is a different kind of buyer and brings a real strength to the deal. Where the landowner is motivated to any degree by a desire to preserve the property, represent the land trust and landowner as partners in conservation: Your land trust is helping the landowner find a realistic way to protect the land while generating some financial return. Even if the landowner has no conservation objectives, it is important to represent yourself as a unique kind of buyer. This can lay the groundwork for an unconventional deal—perhaps a low option consideration or down payment and a long time frame for exercising an option or for closing.

There are many arguments that explain how and why your land trust is a different kind of acquisition partner:

- **Commitment to protection.** The land trust's protection goals drive every transaction. It is committed to the deal for conservation motives and for its reputation, since it puts itself publicly on the line to see the deal through. Cite examples of projects that were completed successfully without large up-front payments.

- **Service.** The land trust provides a real service to the landowner. It brings special skills and works out a unique deal. The land trust can make things happen.

- **Tax advantages.** Transactions with the land trust involving charitable donations offer an economic benefit not available with a conventional buyer.

- **Flexibility and creativity.** The land trust is positioned to work flexibly and creatively to meet the special needs of the landowner. An aspect of the property that may be an impediment to conventional buyers, such as the family's desire to reserve the right to camp on the property during the summer, may not be an impediment for your land trust.

Finding Common Ground

The Black River Conservancy had approached estate trustees about the estate property, which they planned to develop. The trustees told the land trust's project manager to work with their attorney, a litigator who was livid over the "do-gooders" trying to derail the development. At one point, the attorney showed the project manager a slide show of the estate. The attorney, clearly personally attached to the land, waxed eloquent in his presentation. The project manager and he were able to connect on a very personal level about the exceptional beauty of the land. The slide show was a catalyst that brought the attorney and project manager to common (and personal) ground. In subsequent meetings, they constructed a deal that worked for both sides.

Establishing a Partnership

Always try to make the landowner (or the representative you're dealing with) your partner in the deal. Whether your approach focuses on financial considerations or conservation goals, demonstrate to the landowner that you are there to help him, that you seek mutually advantageous goals. By developing his trust and confidence in you personally and in your land trust, you can create a working partnership that will smooth the way to future agreements.

GENERAL PRINCIPLES

You probably negotiate something every day. You bargain for a used car, persuade your children to go to bed, or convince a board member to take the lead on a fundraising campaign. Negotiating a conservation transaction isn't all that different.

Every landowner meeting will be different, but there are important rules of thumb:

- Listen. Try to learn as much as you can about the landowner's interests, needs, motivations, perspectives, and comfort with a proposal.

- Dress appropriately. Appearances are important.

- Be open, positive, professional. Be sensitive to the landowner's needs and interests. Project confidence.

- Take notes. Don't count on your memory to record everything you hear. Notes, particularly of anything that represents an agreement, will be useful when structuring the contract. Taking notes also can reinforce the landowner's feeling that you are a serious buyer.

- Follow up as you say you will. If you don't know how to answer a question, say so, and get back to the landowner with the answer.

Ground Rules for the Negotiation Meeting

When the time arrives to prepare for a substantive meeting with a landowner or representative, you need to focus on some very important details, which may or may not be under your control.

Who are the parties? With whom will you negotiate? What is their authority? What is their professional expertise? How many parties will you be meeting with? Will the landowner bring in an attorney or other professional? Being outnumbered or "out-professionaled" can put you at a disadvantage, or at least a psychological disadvantage. Consider bringing along a team to support you. On the other hand, sometimes you will garner a sort of sympathy if you are obviously outnumbered, undercutting a potentially adversarial approach.

Others Who May Represent
(or Be Present with) Landowners

Brokers. Brokers may have a legitimate role in the transaction for a property that has been listed; on the other hand, they may try to insert themselves into a deal. Brokers ordinarily are paid by the seller a percentage of the sale price. Consequently, they want the highest price possible and they want a deal. The first point can pose a stumbling block: brokers generally are not receptive to a bargain sale. But the second point works in your favor. If brokers see that you are serious about acquiring the land, they will work for you and listen to your concerns.

Attorneys. Attorneys have a different role. They simply protect the landowner's legal interests and generally defend whatever decision the landowner makes. You need to understand the attorney's relationship with the landowner: Is this the landowner's personal attorney or someone brought in to deal with this project? Does the attorney have a longstanding relationship with the landowner? (If so, the attorney will represent the landowner's opinion more authoritatively, and will be harder to get around.) Does the attorney specialize in real estate? Does she work alone, with a small firm, or for a large firm (and what kind of firm)? Has she worked before on conservation transactions? Does she care about or even understand conservation?

Accountants/business managers. Financial experts bring technical expertise to the negotiating table. You definitely should consider bringing your own financial expert if the landowner will have one present.

Offspring. Children can both help and hinder a negotiation. Often, they can articulate what their parents want when the parents cannot. On the other hand, their attention to inheritance prospects may add a complicating element to the negotiations. Be alert to the family dynamics and listen particularly hard to what the children want.

Where and when will you meet? Where and when you meet can influence the outcome of your negotiations (meeting in the office of a landowner's attorney is very different than meeting in a landowner's home). Consider what "spin" the location will give. It's traditional for the seller to set the location for the negotiation—the seller is, after all, the one with most control over the deal—but if you have some choice in the matter, pick a time and place where both of you will feel comfortable (unless your strategy, for some reason, is to make the other party as uncomfortable as possible). Even the smallest logistical detail can have a bearing on your negotiations and itself become something to negotiate.

Faces and Places

The Swan Lake Land Trust had written two letters to ACR Development about their 4,000-acre undeveloped parcel adjoining Swan Lake. The trust hoped to purchase a conservation easement on sensitive areas immediately adjacent to the lake and bordering a creek draining into it.

Finally, Sara Nublin, the executive director, received a call from ACR's director of facilities saying he wanted to discuss sale of the easement. After two phone calls, it appeared that ACR was seriously interested, although they were skeptical about the trust's sophistication and wherewithal, and they evinced no interest in a charitable reduction in the price they expected to receive. "Let's meet to see if we can come to terms," he suggested. "Want to come over here and get together with our tax attorney and executive vice-president?"

Sara discussed the negotiation with her closest adviser on the board, a real estate broker. "No way," he said. "Let's do it here, at our new offices. That way they'll see we're for real, and substantial." He suggested they include their pro bono attorney and most senior "gray hair" from the board to match up with ACR's lineup. As it turns out, the board member knew the CEO of ACR from college days.

The meeting went well. The trust appeared professional and capable. The trust's attorney was able to educate ACR's attorney on the use of easements. The board member was persuasive in selling them on a partial gift. After several weeks of discussion, ACR agreed to give the trust a one-year option to buy an easement at 75 percent of the appraised value.

The negotiation location and team had contributed significantly to the success of the negotiations.

Preparing for the Negotiation

Make sure you are in command of as many of the facts as possible. Analyze the issues so that you have a sense of the motivations of the parties involved.

Prioritize your goals. This will guide your negotiation strategy and help you hold your ground. Know what you want to protect and how you hope to do it. Know your time and cash limits and what terms you can accept. Consider what your initial offer will likely be and how high you can go. Know which goals are more important than others, which you could compromise and which you cannot. This allows you flexibility and latitude in your negotiation.

Think through your upcoming meeting. Where do you want to end up? How can you get there? Consider every angle. Identify "what if" questions you can ask to learn more about the landowner's parameters. Put yourself in the

The Importance of Being Prepared

At its initial meeting with the TORAX Corporation, the Morgan County Land Trust came prepared. Executive Director Rand Tilford had carefully researched the property by reviewing a title report, the county's zoning classifications, and all filings with the county Department of Health. In addition, with the permission of TORAX, he had walked the entire property and photographed key portions.

He learned some interesting things. A notice of foreclosure by a bank had been recorded nine months earlier. The planning records revealed two attempts at subdivision, one of which was abandoned and the other denied after two public hearings. Those records also revealed an environmental assessment that highlighted sensitive wetlands and pervasive drainage problems. There were also references to several buried—and perhaps leaking—fuel tanks.

In the negotiations, TORAX representatives indicated the corporation's notion of the property's value, which was based on assumptions of developability that Rand knew to be unrealistic. Pulling out his files, he politely turned the discussion around: "It is my understanding that development efforts on the property have been frustrated. We would like to work with you based on a realistic notion of the property's capacity and worth."

His research and his understanding of its implications were impressive. He put forth a purchase price that appeared to jar the TORAX representatives. "I'm sorry, but that's all we can prudently pay for the property given its limitations." The TORAX team appeared disgruntled and the meeting ended. Two days later, however, they called back and asked for a meeting. "Maybe we can do something." In fact, they agreed to a sale price close to what the trust proposed.

landowner's shoes as you think through her potential responses. Consider the kinds of questions she will ask and your answers. Write down how you think the negotiation will progress. Run your strategy by a board member, fellow staff member, or other colleague. The more you prepare the better you will be able to respond to surprises. (On the other hand, don't take so much time preparing that the property is sold, or get so set on your strategy that you don't listen during negotiations.)

Some Additional Negotiating Tips

Be patient. Effective negotiating takes time. When you are rushed for time, the other side may sense this and take advantage of it to force the deal they want. You need the leeway to take something away and "think about it," which prompts the other side to think about it, too. Rushing a decision more often than not creates an atmosphere of desperation—certainly not the attitude you want to project.

Assume everything is negotiable.

Maintain your bargaining power. Conceal your lust for a property. Revealing that you must have the property can leave you with little room to negotiate. Don't be deceived by false threats of immediate sale. "We've got eight all-cash offers on this property" sometimes translates into, "We've got nothing, but you don't know this."

Ask for a gift. Always ask for a gift, if the situation is right. If you don't ask, you aren't likely to be offered it!

Protect your interest. Don't be afraid to be tough. Remember that the other side is usually protecting its interests as vigorously; it's your obligation to do the same for your land trust's and the public's interests. Sound business deals keep your land trust healthy and make more deals possible.

Know when to say no. There can be a moment of truth in a negotiation when you have to draw the line, walking away without a deal. Know your land trust's limits.

Get at the "why" behind the landowner's position. If you understand why the landowner is holding out for a certain price, is reluctant to sell the land, or is pressing for a quick closing, you are better able to think of a creative solution that might help the landowner.

Talk in terms of hypotheticals. Use hypothetical discussions to narrow down options the landowner may agree to and what will be out of the question. Use phrases such as: "What if we were able to..." or "If we could do X, would you consider Y?"

Build momentum. Move from agreements that are easy to those that are hard; from those that are verbal to those that are written down. As you gain agreement, you are increasing the investment by the parties. This builds momentum that is critical for reaching agreement on the most difficult aspects of the deal. Once the parties are excited and invested, "deal-breaker" issues may assume a different look than they might at the start of your discussions. Of course, keep in mind that the project's momentum works on you as well as on the landowner.

Maintain flexibility. Because the elements you are negotiating in a transaction are interdependent, maintain your flexibility. Avoid ultimatums. Keep your agreements conditional until you have the entire deal worked out.

Ask for something in return for a concession. Never make a concession without asking for something in return. The other side expects this: it is the underlying premise of negotiations. If the seller asks to stay on the property for

60 days after closing, you might agree and ask for a 60-day extension to the option period or a lower option consideration. (Sometimes, however, it can stand you in good stead to concede some major point early on in the negotiations without asking anything in return. This can change the tenor of the negotiations, removing you from the standard tit-for-tat, and giving you bargaining credit when you really need it.)

Be persistent. No matter how well prepared and professional you are in your efforts, obstacles will arise. These may bring your negotiations to a standstill. Don't be discouraged. Persistence and patience may pay off years later.

Don't negotiate in writing: Confirm in writing. Negotiating in writing has several disadvantages:

- It slows things down (and you lose momentum).

- It is less flexible and more difficult to retract.

- You learn less about the landowner—and the "why" behind his position—since you don't get spontaneous feedback.

- It can move you from a personal to a more formal relationship with the landowner.

There are times, on the other hand, when putting your agreements in writing make sense:

- You want to pin down the conceptual agreements you've reached with the landowner.

- You want to clarify a complex point.

- You are working through a representative and want to be sure the information is reaching the landowner correctly.

- You simply feel more comfortable proceeding this way with a particular landowner.

- You need to say something unpleasant. A letter can give the landowner time to think it over.

Also, sometimes a landowner may request, or a corporation require, that you put the agreement in writing.

Framing the Deal: Negotiating the Basic Terms

Before beginning the process of framing the deal—discussing the basic business aspects of the project—you need to understand the elements that typically are negotiated at the conceptual level before they are described in legal language in an acquisition agreement (these include type of agreement, consideration or down payment to be paid, what exactly will be acquired, purchase price, timing, financing, and major contingencies).

You generally will not have to involve an attorney at this stage.

Form of Contract

Always seek an option as the form of agreement, since it imposes no risk on the land trust other than the payment of a nonrefundable option consideration. A landowner may want to use a purchase-and-sale agreement, which binds the land trust.

The most cogent argument you can offer for why you need an option is its strategic leverage: it provides a concrete protection opportunity with an urgent time frame. You can say to the community, in effect, "our right to buy the property will expire on (date) unless you can help." With a purchase-and-sale agreement, on the other hand, you may lose this sense of urgency. Even though a purchase-and-sale agreement does not assure acquisition—and in fact may be structured to be substantively similar to an option—most people will perceive that the land is protected.

There are many ways to structure an option:

- If the landowner wants to eliminate the immediate costs of property taxes, you can structure the timing and amount of option payments to cover them.

- If the landowner wants to sell now because land values are high, you could consider an option that allows the landowner to continue to market the land. The terms of this kind of agreement might be that the land trust must either exercise its option or drop the deal when the landowner receives another offer.

- If the landowner wants to sell a large property that you cannot afford to purchase all at once, you can offer a phased option: the land trust has an option on the entire property with, say, six months to close on the first portion. If it fails to close on any of the phases, it loses its option on any remaining portions.

Structuring a Phased Option

The land trust signs an option to purchase a 100-acre property for $1,000 an acre. The land trust pays $5,000 as a nonrefundable option consideration to be credited to the purchase price and exercises its option on the first 30 acres, for which the price is $30,000. The land trust pays $30,000 at closing and allocates $5,000 as the option consideration for the next phase. Subsequently, the land trust exercises its option on another 30-acre phase and deposits $30,000 at close of escrow. Again, $5,000 in option consideration has been rolled over for the remaining land. If the land trust fails to close on any of the phases, the landowner keeps the $5,000 and the remaining land.

Estate To Be Acquired

Most likely, you and the landowner will begin negotiations with an idea of what interest in the property the land trust wants to acquire and what interest the landowner is willing to sell. You also should already have considered to what extent your land trust can be flexible in acquiring more or less than your ideal: will acquiring an easement achieve your purposes? Can you afford to purchase the whole property and subsequently sell off the portion that is non-sensitive?

You may have to revisit and revise your agreement on what it is the land trust will acquire if you fail to reach agreement on other aspects of your deal.

Dealing with restrictions. In defining the estate to be acquired, one of the most common issues land trusts will encounter is a request or requirement by a conservation-minded seller that the property be sold subject to some kind of binding restriction, typically contained in the deed. Common restrictions include prohibitions on development and on public access. The desired restrictions may fall right in line with your land trust's protection goals for the property and can help you by lowering the value of the land, but there can be problems.

- Restrictions typically (but not always) will affect the value of the land, thereby reducing the value of any donation the landowner expects to claim for tax purposes and the price a land trust can pay; you need to make sure the landowner understands this.

- Restrictions make it difficult to secure financing.

- Restrictions inhibit your flexibility regarding future use of the land, whether you intend to use the land yourself or sell to a third party.

- Restrictions reduce the threat to the property, making fundraising more difficult.

Don't accept restricted property without the advice of experienced people.

Alternatives to restrictions that might jeopardize the project include a right of first refusal back to the owner if the land trust can't meet its protection goal or limitations on the boundaries or the duration of the restriction. If your project is an agency preacquisition, your land trust can ask the agency to prepare a management plan that addresses the concerns of the landowner. This doesn't necessarily bind the agency, but it may appease the seller.

Consideration/Deposit

When you enter into an option agreement or purchase-and-sale agreement, you generally will need to put money down. The option consideration is generally nonrefundable, and the purchase-and-sale agreement deposit (or earnest money) is usually refundable only if the contingency is not satisfied. How much you put down is negotiable. Landowners frequently want a large down payment, since this offers greater assurance that the deal will go through. Naturally, your land trust will want to keep this as low as possible. An option payment can be as low as $10. Many landowners won't expect a large up-front sum from a nonprofit organization.

Evaluate your capacity to put funds at risk: How much are you willing to lose? What is the likelihood of your completing the acquisition? If you are uncertain, put less at risk or make the payment refundable if contingencies aren't satisfied. Of course, putting up a large consideration can smooth the way with other elements of your agreement, making the landowner feel more comfortable that the deal will close and giving you leverage in lowering the eventual purchase price.

The following are arguments for a low initial payment.

- *Commitment.* The real value your land trust offers the landowner is its commitment and ability to make the deal happen: managing the logistics, mustering public support, raising funds. This is the consideration—value— in addition to money paid by the land trust.

- *Limited funds.* The land trust has limited funds that must be stretched over a variety of land protection projects. (Don't say, "we don't have money," which will undercut your credibility.)

- *Cost of completing projects.* Point out that to complete the project, the land trust will be investing lots of cash for standard transaction costs as well as special costs (such as fundraising campaigns and site management plans). This is part of your commitment to the project.

- *Broker comparison.* While the land trust isn't a broker, in some respects it provides services of similar value, which benefit the landowner. The land trust gives the landowner access to a special market and special funding.

- *"Fiduciary" obligation.* As a public benefit organization, supported directly by donations and indirectly through favorable tax consideration, it is a good policy to avoid the appearance of placing large sums of money at risk.

- *Deal-breaker.* Large sums up front are, quite simply, deal-breakers for your land trust.

You can strengthen any of these arguments if you can back yourself up with examples of past acquisitions where you paid little up front.

Other strategies. If despite your best arguments it's clear that the landowner requires substantial up-front money, you might keep payments manageable if you get to the heart of why the landowner needs the money.

- *Stretch out payment over time.* If the landowner needs a steady stream of payments, you can structure an option in the form of monthly installments.

- *Make payment refundable under a wide range of conditions.* Sometimes all the landowner wants is the money in the bank now, regardless of the chances of having to refund it. Consider the impediments to your completing the deal (such as subdivision approval or legislative appropriations) and make your deposit refundable if these conditions are not satisfied.

- *Make payment a loan.* If the landowner is strapped for cash and less concerned about your commitment to the deal, consider making a loan as consideration for the agreement, meeting the needs of the landowner and keeping your risks at a minimum. If you purchase the property, the funds can be credited to the purchase price. If you don't purchase the property, the funds can be deemed loaned to the landowner and must be repaid according to a schedule.

- *Tie payment to interest in property.* Consider making the payment attributable to an interest in the property (such as a 10 percent undivided interest in the land or a lot, if the property is subdivided) so that even if you cannot close on the entire property, you do not lose your investment.

The Ten-Dollar Option

The Lower Walker Valley Land Trust aims to acquire easements on or fee title to lands bordering the Lower Walker River and Walker Lake. Through a successful fundraising program and sale of lands to the state fish and wildlife commission, the trust has succeeded in saving six properties.

Now, a national timber company has declared surplus a 4,000-acre parcel on the river. The company has listed the property with a local broker for a bulk sale price of $9,000,000, based on the value of the property once subdivided and developed. At the initial meeting with the company, the land trust indicated interest. They believed they could sell much of the land to the federal government to augment a national forest. The balance they could sell for private housing, subject to a land-use plan and conservation easements. This would take up to five years.

"We'll pay you the $9,000,000, but we will have to acquire the property in phases over five years. We'll need an option over the property, and we typically pay $10 for option consideration."

At this point the company representative nearly fell from his chair. "Ten dollars, are you serious?" The land trust explained that this was how they operated, that they didn't have major liquid resources, but if they had site control over the property, they could put into motion their substantial army of fundraisers and friends. Without an option, no one would take the opportunity seriously. The trust gave the representative the names of other landowners who had granted $10 options.

It worked. The trust got an option on the property for $10 that would terminate if they failed to acquire specified amounts of land each year.

Building in Adequate Time

Time can be every bit as critical to your deal as money. You need time to secure funding, complete your inspections, and so on. You need a buffer against inevitable delays. The ideal is a long-term option or, in the case of a purchase-and-sale agreement, a long period between down payment and closing. You want as much time as you can get; the landowner, however, may become nervous if you ask for too much time.

Be sure you've thought through a workable time line. While you can always hope to negotiate extensions at a later date—and a long option term to start with gives you more time to do this—don't count on it.

You might be able to identify advantages to the owner of holding the property longer. Perhaps she can realize rent or other income from the land during the option period. If the market is on an upswing the landowner might get a better price from some other buyer at the end of the option term if the land trust is unable to complete the deal.

Putting Time on Your Side

Friends of the Swamp had been in discussions with the Alou family for months about purchase of a critical wetlands buffer. The terms were basically agreed upon: The Friends would pay $100 for an option, and acquire the property for 50 percent of its appraised fair market value. The only open issue was the length of the option period.

The Alou family said they could only hold the property off the market for six months. The Friends knew this wasn't long enough. Their source of funding was a state-managed mitigation fund, which was projected to generate funds twelve to eighteen months later in connection with a highway extension project.

So the Friends found a solution that met both parties' needs. They would acquire a six-month option. If at the end of that period the Friends could produce reliable evidence that the funding would be available in the next six months, or if they would pay $5,000 (to be credited against the purchase price), the Alou family would extend the option for six additional months. At the end of that period, the Friends could extend the option period for an additional six months by paying $10,000 (to be credited against the purchase price). The result? The Friends obtained site control for up to 18 months. The Alous had the assurance that if the Friends' project plans weren't coming together they could sell the property to another buyer.

As it turned out, the Friends needed the first six-month extension period, and they were able to get it by showing a written confirmation from the state of the availability of the mitigation funds.

Achieving the Right Price

One of your major negotiating points will always be the price. Your land trust needs to consider not only what is affordable, but what is appropriate. Paying too much can open your land trust to criticism that you're wasting money and make it more difficult to negotiate good deals in the future.

Because price is frequently (though not always) the biggest sticking point, it's often best to postpone this discussion until you have reached agreement on other aspects of the deal. If the landowner wants to talk price early on, keep your agreements tentative, pointing out that your ability to meet the desired price will depend on the other terms of the deal. (On the other hand, if you reach an early agreement on price, you frequently will find that subsequent agreements are easier.)

Price can be specified in a variety of ways:

- as a fixed sum (this is the most common)

- as an amount changing—usually increasing—over time determined by formula, for example: (1) a percentage of fair market value as determined by an appraisal or (2) a dollar amount per acre tied to a survey that establishes the exact acreage (the parties can establish floors [minimums] or ceilings [maximums] on the price)

Making Your Offer

How and when you make your offer varies with the circumstances of the deal, the character of the landowner, your personal style, and the preferences and practices of your land trust. There is no one right way or time. Some prefer to present extreme offers, then dicker; others present and stick with a carefully thought-out offer. Do what feels comfortable for you and what makes sense under the circumstances, but don't do it without a strategy.

What a property is worth can be an extremely sensitive issue that frequently is tied to the landowner's ego. Talk about price in terms of what you can afford, not what the property is worth.

All Cash versus Seller Financing

Most sellers will want to be paid in full in cash at closing; this puts money in their hands immediately and avoids the uncertainty and administrative difficulties of financing. Landowners frequently will accept a lower price if they get an all-cash deal. On the other hand, landowners may consider financing the deal for a variety of reasons:

- They may assume that they will have to take back at least a portion of the purchase price as a note secured by a mortgage since, as a rule, it is difficult for any buyer to secure financing for raw land.

- The landowner may be willing to provide financing in return for a higher price.

- A landowner might find it financially attractive to take back a note, making it an installment sale whereby capital gain will be recognized over a period of years, thus delaying or reducing taxes.

- Some landowners like the idea of getting money from the property over time, something like a pension plan.

- If the landowner is under pressure to sell quickly and you need financing to proceed with the deal, he may be willing to provide it.

Seller financing usually is not available for property sold through foreclosure or at auction.

If the seller is providing financing, at this stage of negotiations you will preliminarily discuss various aspects of it, such as:

- amount of down payment (the balance of the price being the amount to be financed)

- interest rate

- security (only if the seller raises the issue at this point), which is usually a mortgage

- repayment schedule and terms

The following may be agreed on at this time or when you draft your agreement:

- whether the obligation becomes due if the property is sold to another party

- right to prepay the note prior to the stated installment dates without penalties

- partial release provisions, by which the seller agrees to release the mortgage or portions of the property if the note is paid down

- substitution of security; that is, allowing the buyer to substitute a new form of security (such as a letter of credit) for the original security (usually a mortgage)

Establishing the Major Contingencies

You can make your obligation to buy a property contingent on certain facts or events. Generally, the more risk involved in the deal—the higher the down payment or purchase price, the less certain you are of conditions such as contamination, the tighter the time lines—the more contingencies you may want to include. Landowners, of course, prefer fewer contingencies (unless they benefit the landowner).

A Clean Offer

The Hudson Trust found itself in an enviable position. An elderly bene-factor pledged a gift of $500,000 to finance purchase of a riverfront parcel for public recreational access. Moreover, the trust had just the property in mind, a two-acre parcel they had been eyeing for several years. Word in the community was that the owner had been stymied in her attempts to sell the property; two successive potential buyers had made contingent offers and had backed away when they saw the difficulties ahead in obtaining devel-opment approvals.

The trust decided to make a clean offer, figuring that the owner would be willing to accept less money for a sure deal. The trust offered $450,000, which was $100,000 less than the developers had offered. The trust's offer was clean, however, the only contingencies being delivery of marketable title and a clean environmental assessment. There was no contingency for obtain-ing financing or for obtaining development approvals.

The landowner balked at first over the price, but eventually agreed to sell at $475,000. The clean offer had been too attractive to resist.

If you know of major contingencies that you will need to incorporate, bring them up early in the negotiations. In general, negotiate contingencies for any-thing about which you don't have 100 percent knowledge at the time of the negotiation, since in most cases you won't do exhaustive "due diligence" inves-tigations until you've got a signed deal.

Common contingencies include:

- securing financing

- obtaining necessary permits and approvals

- establishing that the property is uncontaminated (see Chapter 14, "Environmental Assessment")

- satisfaction with the state of title (see Chapter 12, "Title")

- price (that is, the price is contingent on a survey, appraisal, or approvals; for example, you might agree on a price of $20,000 if the property passes a percolation test for a septic system, $10,000 if it doesn't)

- land trust board approval

Anything in your agreement can be made conditional and many conditions can be subjective. For example, you could make the agreement conditional on your land trust "finding in its absolute discretion that the property is suitable for its needs." (Although a seller could object mightily to such an open-ended out for the buyer.)

Chapter 10

FINAL NEGOTIATIONS: WRITING DOWN THE AGREEMENT

Once you reach oral agreement on the basic business elements, move as quickly as possible to a preliminary draft of your acquisition agreement. Circumstances change constantly: competing offers may be made, the landowner's financial situation may change, the landowner may die.

In this draft, you confirm conceptual agreements in legal language and identify the remaining terms to be negotiated (by inserting suggested language).

At this point in the negotiations, the landowner generally will be cooperative. You can ask to see copies of any documents the landowner may have, including title report, environmental assessments, or deeds. The information these provide, and the language used, can help you draft the agreement.

With any luck, this stage of negotiations will go smoothly, especially if you work with standard forms and have a clear understanding with the landowner. But it can be prolonged:

- It's time-consuming to generate a sound legal agreement. Generally, you will have a number of important business elements to hammer out.

- Your deal may run aground on some of the final elements.

- Putting agreements in writing may cause either party to rethink the agreement.

- Either party may need to get approvals before the document can be signed.

Deciding Who Will Prepare the First Draft

Consider who is in the best position to prepare the first draft inexpensively and quickly. It is generally to your land trust's advantage to do this, since you can write up any ambiguities in your land trust's favor and work with forms that you're familiar with. But if the landowner really wants to do it, preparing the first draft can help him feel in control, which might work well for both of you. Generally, the more sophisticated the landowner, the more likely that he will want an attorney to prepare the first draft.

If you haven't involved an attorney yet, do so at this stage. Some land trust representatives have enough real estate experience that they can negotiate and draft the fine points of the agreement, but nothing in writing should go out without review by an attorney.

"If We Had Just Thought This Out..."

Save Our Trees, a local land trust in Oregon, had solved a boiling dispute between loggers and environmentalists by agreeing to purchase Rapacious Lumber's six-mile creek tract of forest land, comprising 600 acres. In negotiating the purchase agreement, RL requested the right to do limited logging on the parcel. In its hurry to sign the agreement before a scheduled press conference, Save our Trees agreed to a provision allowing RL to log a specified amount of board feet of timber, representing a small fraction of the timber on the property.

After the press conference and the euphoria it spawned had faded, RL went to work. In five days of nonstop cutting, RL took down the permitted board feet by clearcutting a prominent hillside.

The community was outraged. Save Our Trees was outraged. But RL insisted that it had complied with letter of the agreement, which did not specify the rate or distribution or timing of the cutting. It was too late.

NEGOTIATING THE FINE POINTS

At this stage of the negotiating, you will finalize the agreement on the following points.

Estate To Be Acquired

The acquisition agreement specifies what rights, improvements, and personal property the buyer will acquire along with the property and describes any restrictions. An exact definition of these is crucial, since the seller is obligated to convey only the agreed-upon rights.

If you are acquiring less than full interest (or acquiring land subject to a restriction such as a covenant or easement limiting use), agreeing on the exact language can be one of the most difficult parts of your negotiation. You have to think of every eventuality and negotiate every word. For instance, if the seller is retaining a life tenancy, you will likely have to negotiate such items as who will handle maintenance and repairs. A change of one or two words can significantly alter the rights being conveyed (potentially affecting both the value of the land and your land trust's ability to protect it).

Consideration/Deposit

The acquisition agreement spells out how the option consideration or purchase-and-sale deposit will be transferred, whether delivered to the landowner or held in escrow; whether the option consideration is applicable to the purchase price; and conditions under which the consideration or deposit can be refunded, if any.

In a purchase-and-sale agreement, the deposit is conventionally considered applicable to the purchase price. In an option agreement, however, there are no conventions.

If your option payment or deposit is significant, it's a good idea to have the payment held in escrow to ensure compliance with the agreement's terms.

Timing

Negotiate specific dates and provisions. With options, you need to establish the term, the time between exercising the option and closing the purchase, and provisions for extensions of both the option term and closing date. With purchase-and-sale agreements, consider the length of time between entering into the agreement and closing, and provisions for extension of the closing.

Both options and purchase-and-sale agreements will likely include time frames for contingencies related to your due diligence activities, such as obtaining a financing commitment within 30 days or procuring a satisfactory title report at least 60 days before closing. The seller generally wants contingencies to expire as quickly as possible, while the buyer wants to allow for termination of the agreement if contingencies are not met.

When specifying time frames, put in hedges such as an extension of the option expiration date or deferred closing. Extensions may be at the buyer's discretion or may be conditioned upon certain things happening. Commonly, the seller will require compensation for the extension, but it may be only a modest amount.

Make sure that key dates don't fall on weekends, holidays, personal vacation days, or at the busy end-of-the-year period.

Terms of Seller Financing

If the seller has agreed to finance the sale, the acquisition agreement outlines basic elements of the financing package: the amount of purchase price to be financed, term of the loan, interest rate, schedule for repaying the principal amount, and security. (See Chapter 16, "Loans.")

The most precise way to include financing terms in your acquisition agreement is to attach the promissory note (see Chapter 16), completed but not yet signed. Often, however, the promissory note is not drawn up until closing and its terms are merely summarized in the acquisition agreement.

Negotiating a nonrecourse loan. The security for the note is critical and can be subject to much negotiation. It is always best—but frequently hard—to get a "nonrecourse" loan from the seller. A nonrecourse loan is one in which the lender recoups only the security if the borrower defaults; the borrower has no personal liability. Following are arguments that might help you:

- The land trust is committed to the deal and therefore likely to pay.

- Recourse indebtedness is identified in the annual audit, sending a signal that may worry funders, members, and donors, undermining the effectiveness of the land trust.

- With its public reputation at stake, the only way the land trust wouldn't pay is in the unlikely event that the land trust goes bankrupt, and in that case the landowner wouldn't gain anything.

- If the seller believes the land is worth the selling price, she should feel secure, since the value of the security will exceed the amount of the loan.

Strategies for encouraging a nonrecourse loan include:

- Put down a sizable down payment (the larger the down payment, the lower the loan and the better the loan-to-value ratio).

- Put up other nonsensitive land owned by the land trust as collateral.

- Have your board members individually guarantee the loan.

While it's always advisable to seek a nonrecourse loan, there are times when the risk you assume in a recourse loan is negligible and you can cede on this point to great advantage, getting other terms that you want in the deal.

Title

Several title issues are subject to negotiation and are usually discussed when drafting the agreement. While it's ideal to have a title report before you sign the acquisition agreement, you frequently won't. The agreement needs to anticipate problems and define remedies. Specifically, the agreement usually describes the following:

- title exceptions: what problems with or qualifications to the seller's ownership must be legally removed (and by whom), and what are acceptable

- type of title insurance and who is responsible for getting it

- type of deed used to convey the property (because of the variance among and complexity of deeds, your attorney should always be involved with deed considerations)

The agreement also may include a provision to adjust the purchase price to reflect the cost of remedying any title problems.

Usually, reaching agreement on which title exceptions to remove and who will do it is fairly straightforward. Sellers, however, tend to be afraid of how much it might cost and may want the right to walk away from the transaction if they cannot remove an exception. It's best if you can make your agreement contingent on clear title but retain the right to accept the property with title flaws. (See Chapter 12, "Title.")

Environmental Liability

The critical issue of environmental (toxic) liability is handled as a combination of representations, warranties, and indemnities and is one of the most highly negotiated facets of modern real estate transactions. You typically will negotiate:

- who will be responsible for any environmental assessment undertaken

- who will be responsible for clean-up, if needed, and what the time frames and price ceilings for this may be

- conditions under which your land trust can walk away from the deal

- who will bear the risk of liability and expense in the future

The land trust wants the seller to make representations about the environmental conditions (preferably about the absence of contamination!) on the site, to provide and pay for an environmental assessment, and to indemnify the land trust against future liabilities and costs arising from the presence of contamination at or before the time of the sale. The seller will want to limit the scope of the representations, the cost of assessment, and liabilities for environmental contamination. There are no formulas here. This is the stuff of hearty negotiation. Have your attorney carefully evaluate the land trust's rights and liabilities. (See Chapter 14, "Environmental Assessment.")

Seller's Covenants, Representations, and Warranties

The buyer can rely on representations and warranties. These serve to flesh out information that is important to the buyer, and the buyer may be able to seek damages from the seller due to an inaccurate representation. Information that is warranted often is not covered by the title report, and in many instances the title insurance specifically excludes these issues from coverage. For example: regular title insurance coverage does not insure that there is access to the property, that there is not trespass or illegal possession of a portion of the property (squatters, use of a trail) that is not of record, or that legal or administrative action is not pending or threatened.

Through representations, you are trying to get the seller to tell you everything he knows about the property that could affect its value and your willingness to buy. These include:

- Seller has the full authority to enter into the agreement. (This representation is particularly important when you are dealing with an entity, such as a trust, estate, partnership, or corporation.)

- The conveyance of the property in accordance with the agreement will not violate state or local subdivision laws.

- The property has vehicular access to a public road.

- No one other than the seller will be in possession of any portion of the property at the close of escrow other than as disclosed in the agreement.

- No suit or other proceeding pending against the property or the seller exists that could affect the seller's title, affect the property's value, or subject the property's owner to liability other than as disclosed in the agreement.

- No current or impending liens or public notices, such as back taxes, will affect the property.

- The property does not pose an environmental threat, it has not been and is not used to store hazardous substances, and no past or present activity has occurred on the property that might result in environmental contamination. (See Chapter 14, "Environmental Assessment.")

- Neither the execution of the agreement nor its consummation will constitute a breach or default under any agreement to which the seller or the property is bound.

- There are no unrecorded easements.

Usually, you will want a clause that will indemnify you against losses or legal claims as a result of any problems with the seller's representations or warranties. If a problem is discovered before closing, the seller should be required to remedy it; failing that, the buyer can terminate the agreement and recover any damages suffered as a result of the representation being untrue. If the problem is discovered after closing, the representations should "survive" closing and the seller should be responsible for any damages you suffer as a result of the untrue representation.

Other Provisions

Right to inspect property. Try to negotiate a condition that allows you to inspect the property. Some sellers (particularly those who suspect problems on their land) are nervous about having you poking around the property, but a land trust should not acquire land that it has not physically inspected.

The right to inspect the property frequently is tied into your negotiations on representations about environmental contamination. The right to inspect also is important to completion of any survey or appraisal and to assuring prior to closing that terms of the deal have been met.

Recording a memorandum or notice of agreement. The acquisition agreement frequently states whether or not the agreement will be recorded. It is good policy to record agreements. This puts potential buyers on notice of your pre-existing rights. Instead of recording the whole agreement, which is long and could publicly disclose information that you would prefer not to disclose (such as price), consider using a memorandum of agreement (or memorandum of option), which is a standard document. The memorandum states that the land trust has an agreement or option to purchase the property. Recording the memorandum of agreement puts the world on notice that the land trust has a contract to buy the property. (The landowner may resist the idea of recording the agreement, since this effectively puts a cloud on title.)

Real estate broker. If a broker is involved in the deal in any way, you will need to specify who will be responsible for paying the broker's fees. Because it can be unclear whether or not a broker was involved in a deal—a broker may have been involved with the property years ago and may step in at the last minute and claim a commission—most contracts include standard language that says a party will indemnify the other party against any broker's claims based on the first party's actions.

Default and Remedies

Negotiation of default and remedies is usually handled by lawyers. At issue is what rights (remedies) one party has if the other defaults, that is, fails to perform its obligations under the agreement. For example, assume a land trust has an agreement to purchase a property from a landowner and the landowner decides not to complete the sale at the last minute because she thinks she has agreed to a price that is too low. The landowner is in default. What remedies does your land trust have? That depends on the agreement or, if the agreement is silent, on state law.

Typically, the land trust will want the right to recover damages. It will also want the right to "specific performance," by which a court can require the landowner to convey the property as stipulated in the contract. The seller, of course, will typically seek similar remedies. Either party can agree that the other party's damages will be limited to a specific dollar amount, commonly called "liquidated damages." Provisions establishing remedies are highly technical and should be reviewed or crafted by your attorney.

Do You Really Have Site Control?

While purchase-and-sale agreements and options are binding contracts, they can, like all contracts, be broken. Consider the following real example:

A landowner, who had given a land trust an option (for which he received $10) to purchase his property for $25,000, turned around and sold the property to a developer for $35,000. While the land trust could have sued the landowner, the courts, under relevant state law, would not have ordered the land to be returned to the landowner, and then deeded to the land trust, since the option had never been recorded and the developer could not be held responsible. Since the land, not damages, was what was important to the land trust, the trust simply walked away having learned a painful lesson.

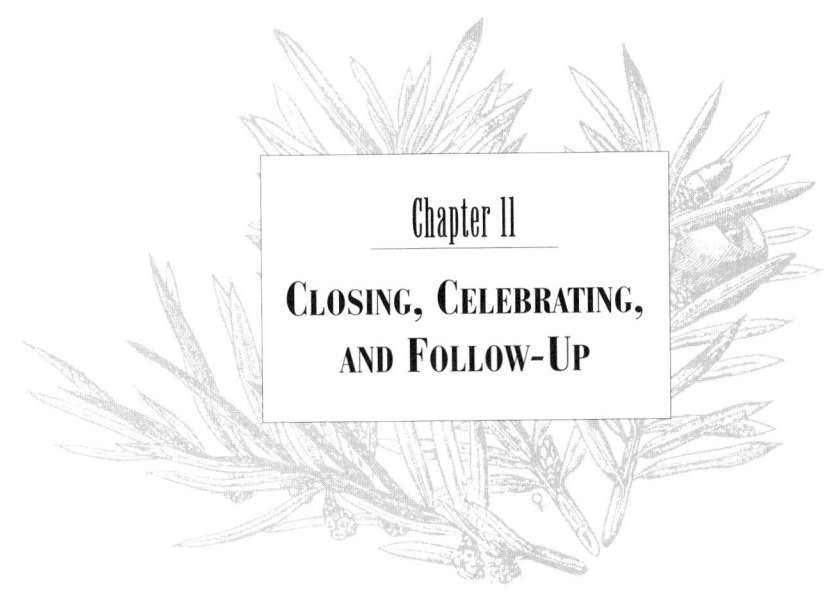

Chapter 11

CLOSING, CELEBRATING, AND FOLLOW-UP

When the acquisition agreement is signed and your funding is in place, you've reached the final stage of your project. What remains is closing the deal according to the terms of the agreement and completing all follow-up tasks: project evaluation, thank-yous, publicity, and celebration.

CLOSING THE DEAL

"Closing" the deal is the culmination of the acquisition, the point at which ownership of the land is transferred to your land trust. This occurs when all the conditions of the acquisition agreement have been satisfied, the buyer has received legal title to the land, and the seller has received the agreed-upon compensation.

While closing is strictly a technical process with very specific steps, it almost always confirms two truisms: first, things generally get put off until the last minute. Second, something is bound to go wrong. The combination can be deadly.

Responsibilities of Closing

Closing requires meticulous, detail-oriented attention to preparing and reviewing the acquisition documents and managing the sequence of delivering these documents to the right parties. Your job is to review and confirm that every document accurately reflects the terms of the agreement, for example that:

- The property description in the title policy is accurate.

- The property description in the conveyance deed is accurate.

- The escrow instructions reflect all agreements.

- The closing statement reflects all agreements about allocation of costs.

After the deal closes, you need to make sure you receive all originals (such as the title policy and deed) and file these appropriately.

Your real estate attorney is the best one to handle the closing technicalities. Nonetheless, as the one most familiar with the guts of the deal, you need to stay involved, particularly when the deal is complex or when there have been lengthy renegotiations and revisions (besides, two heads always are better than one when it comes to double-checking). Be explicit about who will do what so nothing slips through the cracks.

Last Minute Surprises

The Canyon Conservancy was on the brink of closing its acquisition of a critical viewshed parcel. The agreements were signed, an escrow opened with the local title company, and the funding was in place. The contract required closing by June 30, and everything seemed in order. On the 28th, the landowner, Avrim Helms, drove into town to sign the deed and other papers at the title company. "Is your wife coming in?" the escrow officer asked. "My wife?" Avrim queried. "I own this land." The escrow officer explained that this was a community property law state, and his wife had a legal interest in the property even though she didn't show up on the chain of title.

Avrim's wife was in Europe, traveling with her daughter. Suddenly the closing was imperiled, especially when Avrim let slip that his wife didn't think too much of this deal.

Fortunately, an experienced title officer knew what to do. Ms. Helms was tracked down in Belgium, where she signed the deed in front of the American Counsel, who attested to her signature. The deed was sent by overnight mail back to the title company, and the transaction closed on time.

Transferring Ownership

Exactly how land ownership is transferred varies state by state according to custom and state law. Usually, closing is tied to the recording of the deed. In some states, however, closing takes place at the moment the deed is delivered to and accepted by the buyer and the funds are delivered to the seller, which may occur prior to recording the deed. The process may be handled by attorneys, realtors, or title companies, through an escrow arrangement or a face-to-face meeting at which the parties review the documents and transfer the deed and funds. Escrow closings are customary in western states; "sit-down" closings are customary in eastern states. Local real estate brokers and attorneys can provide information and advice about procedures in your area.

Escrow

Escrow is a legal arrangement between two or more parties whereby certain instruments or property will be placed with a third party, the escrow agent, for safekeeping for a set period of time, pending the fulfillment of a condition or performance of a specified act.

Escrow agent. The escrow agent is any person engaged in the business of managing escrows and is usually designated by agreement of buyer and seller in the purchase agreement. Generally, the title company fulfills this role, holding both the deed and the purchase money until all conditions of the contract are fulfilled. However, any lawyer, licensed institution, or broker may act as an escrow agent, depending on the laws and customs of the area.

The escrow agent plays a crucial, neutral role. According to the law in most states, the escrow agent has a fiduciary relationship with both the buyer and seller, which means the agent must protect the best financial interests of both parties. The agent carries out the escrow instructions given by both parties, and escrow closes only when the agent can comply with the instructions.

Because of the escrow agent's neutrality, he can perform a number of valuable services to keep a deal moving forward. These include getting the preliminary title report, prorating and paying taxes due, transferring insurance between the two parties, making sure documents are in proper order, filing papers with the proper local agencies, making sure title insurance is issued, and preparing a closing statement.

Escrow instructions. Escrow instructions are the ground rules for the escrow agent. They follow the terms of the contract of sale and constitute a separate agreement, binding the parties legally. These instructions may be either the agent's preprinted form instructions (these are common for residential real estate transactions) or customized instructions. The latter may be either unilateral, in which a separate set of instructions is written out by each party and given to the escrow agent, or bilateral, in which one set of instructions is drafted and signed by both parties. (Frequently, the land trust will draft the joint escrow instructions.)

Regardless of the style of closing, a closing statement is prepared. This statement is the accounting of funds in the real estate sale and is provided to both the buyer and seller. The statement shows how much money was involved, what services were rendered, and who paid for each of these services. It is, in effect, your snapshot of the entire transaction from a financial point of view. (It's a good idea for internal accounting purposes to require closing statements for all transactions.) The statement may be prepared either by the escrow agent, if the closing is handled through escrow, by the parties' attorneys, or by a broker involved in the transaction.

There are a number of fees and other expenses associated with closing, many of which vary depending on the state where the transaction takes place.

These include:

- escrow fees

- recording fees

- taxes (transfer taxes, prorated property taxes, compensatory taxes resulting from termination of a preferential tax classification, back taxes)

- notary fees

- title insurance premium

- broker's fees

Example of Closing Statement

A simplified closing statement would look something like this:

	Seller		Buyer	
	Debit	Credit	Debit	Credit
Real property		$80,000	$80,000	
Prepaid taxes		$1,500	$1,500	
Sales commission	$4,500			
Escrow fee			$150	
Title insurance premium			$300	
Cash paid by buyer to close				$81,950
Cash received by seller	$77,000			
Totals	$81,500	$81,500	$81,950	$81,950

This sample statement tells you:

- The seller sold the land (the real property in line one) for $80,000. He also received a credit of $1,500 because the seller had prepaid taxes for the period following closing, for which the buyer must reimburse the seller. This gave the seller a positive balance of (the seller was due) $81,500. However, under the terms of the escrow agreement, the seller had to pay his broker a sales commission of $4,500. Thus, the seller walked away from the deal with $77,000.

- The buyer paid out $80,000 for the land. She also paid out $1,500 for the taxes, $150 for a surveyor's fee, and $300 for a title insurance policy. This means that the buyer laid out a total of $81,950 to acquire title.

This example is simplified. There usually would be more entries on it, depending upon the actual closing costs involved.

WRAPPING UP

As you close the acquisition, you simultaneously prepare for an equally important aspect of completing your project: the thank-yous, publicity, and celebration.

Thank those who helped. When the project is done, thank everyone you worked with. This includes the landowner and his attorney, key community supporters, the staff or volunteers who worked with you, agency staff (if the project is a preacquisition), and title company staff. Recognize the efforts of those who helped and they will be more willing to help in the future.

Get media coverage. While you should have planned your publicity well in advance of the closing, now is the time to put out a press release and, if appropriate, invite the press to your celebration. Naturally, you need to carefully consider what you say, particularly if you encountered sensitive or controversial issues.

Celebrate! Depending on the circumstances, your celebration may be an in-house celebration for your land trust and supporters or a formal, public celebration that showcases the land and those who made the project happen. This is your opportunity to give credit publicly to the landowner and others whose support was critical and to raise the profile of your land trust.

Evaluate. As a final step, sit down with your key project team members and review all phases of the project. Compare your original project budget to the actual expenditures. Critique your strategic approach and consider what you might do differently next time. Discuss ways to work together more efficiently. There's no better way to learn.

Section III

DUE DILIGENCE STEPS

Τ his section explains some of the technical aspects of land ownership and real estate transactions, and the steps you should take to minimize risks associated with them. These matters can be critical. You will likely need the help of profession als, who may be willing to donate or discount their services.

Chapter 12

TITLE

T he term "title" means evidence of ownership—that is, the legal documentation of an owner's right to the property. Before you commit to acquire land or easements, you want to make sure there are no title problems that could limit the owner's ability or right to sell the property freely or could unacceptably restrict your use of the property. In legal language, this is called "free from major title defects."

Title matters can be extraordinarily murky. Establishing a clear understanding of who owns what, and under what conditions, can tax the resources even of specialists. Examining the "state of title" on a property involves determining all those who own rights associated with the land and what form of proof they have to establish ownership. Clearly, this is a vital part of any land or easement acquisition, helping you:

- identify the right party to talk to (sometimes landowners are confused about what they own or have forgotten that there are co-owners)

- confirm that the land trust will be able to acquire all necessary uses (a prior deed restriction prohibiting public picnicking could render the property useless for your land trust's purposes, if public access is part of your acquisition criteria)

- more accurately estimate value (if, for example, all mineral rights are reserved, the value of the property may be greatly reduced)

LAND OWNERSHIP: AN OVERVIEW

Under the law, owning land is viewed as holding a "bundle of rights" that can be divided and shared among a number of parties. These rights include the right to possess, occupy, use, and enjoy the land; the right to remove resources; the right to exclude others from the land; and the right to sell, lease, or will all or part of these rights.

It is rare for a landowner to own the entire bundle of rights. Typically, as property changes hands over the years, previous owners and third parties will retain or be granted various interests, such as access easements or rights to minerals. In addition, these parties may share certain rights at specific times. For example, a landowner might lease his land for a certain period, thereby ceding certain rights, such as occupancy, during that time. Or, a landowner might grant a neighbor an access easement specific to certain times of the day or year.

LEGAL ISSUES AFFECTING TITLE

The quality of title to property can be "diminished," or compromised, in a variety of ways. The first way is through an encumbrance, which is any right or interest in a piece of land other than an ownership or tenancy interest. There are two basic types of encumbrances: those that relate to the use of the property (including covenants, conditions, and easements) and liens.

Encumbrances require detailed analysis. They can affect the owner's ability or willingness to sell and price she is willing to accept or, on the other side, the suitability of the property for the land trust. For example, a recorded covenant limiting the use of a piece of property might seriously impact the selling price of the property (though it would not alter the owner's ability to sell the property to any interested party).

Liens

The four most common types of liens are monetary, mechanics', tax, and judgment liens.

Monetary liens. Monetary liens are commonly referred to as mortgages or deeds of trust. Like all liens, they need to be resolved before title to a property can change hands. Whenever an owner secures new loans with the same piece of property, the property may be encumbered with multiple liens: first, second, third, or even fourth mortgages. Normally, in the case of default, the holders of subsequent liens against a property cannot collect until the holder of the first lien has been paid in full. The seller usually pays off mortgages prior to or at the time of selling the property, although the buyer may agree to assume an existing loan as part of the purchase consideration.

Mechanics' liens. Under the laws of some states, any party who performs work or furnishes materials in the construction or repair of real estate improvements can file a mechanics' lien if the bills for the work or materials have not been paid in a timely manner. The lien is against the specific piece of real property on which the work has been performed and cannot be applied against the rest of the debtor's assets. Usually, state law provides that if the lien is not paid within a certain time period (for example, ninety days), the claimant must file a mechanics' lien foreclosure suit. If a lien is placed on the property, the debtor is usually given one year to pay off the lien and still retain title.

Tax liens and assessments. As the name implies, tax liens come about whenever a federal, state, or local government has a claim against a property as the result of unpaid taxes. The type of tax delinquency may affect the seller's overall situation and flexibility.

Tax Liens

A *federal tax lien* results from unpaid federal income, estate, or gift taxes. An income tax lien is a general lien against the real and personal property of a taxpayer; an estate tax lien is a lien against the decedent's estate.

A *state tax lien* for unpaid inheritance taxes is a specific lien against inherited property. Depending on state law, when property is sold by the estate during probate, it may not be subject to the lien for state inheritance taxes in the hands of the new owner; it will be subject, however, to any lien for unpaid federal estate taxes.

Some states have *property tax liens* that are specific liens against real property on which property taxes are due and unpaid. In most of the states that have these liens, if the lien is not paid off within a certain time, the property can be seized and sold at public auction.

For some properties, a *special assessment*, or special tax, may also exist. This is an occasional tax levied against a property to meet expenses incurred in connection with a public improvement such as widening a street, dredging a canal, laying in a sewer line, or acquiring open space. The property remains subject to the assessment lien regardless of changes in ownership. This is of particular importance in cases where your land trust is offered land as a gift. If special assessments are in effect, your land trust may be obligated to pick up the hidden price tag.

Judgment liens. Judgment liens result from the final determination of the rights of parties in a legal action, such as a divorce proceeding. When one party sues another and is awarded monetary damages, the winning party becomes the judgment creditor, while the loser becomes the judgment debtor. In some states, when the judgment creditor records the judgment, it creates a lien upon all of the losing party's property in that county (subject to certain exemptions provided by statute). To collect the judgment, the judgment creditor can then request that the debtor's property be seized and sold at public auction.

Easements

An easement is the right to enter and use another person's property for some special purpose. Most easements are *appurtenant easements*. These restrict, or "burden," a specific parcel of land and benefit a specific parcel of land, such as a driveway easement across a parcel of land that benefits the neighboring, land-locked parcel of land. Appurtenant easements define the relationship between two pieces of land, rather than between two individual owners, and are transferred with the land when it is sold to a new owner. Some easements benefit a person or organization, and not land. These are known in law as *easements in gross*. For example, a utility easement conveys certain rights to and benefits the utility company, not an adjacent piece of land.

How Easements Are Created

Express easements are freely granted by one party to another party, usually in the form of a deed. If recorded, such easements will show up on a title search.

Implied easements are judged to exist, even though they are not written down and will not be disclosed by a title report. For example, if someone buys a parcel in a residential subdivision that includes recreational areas, the right to use those areas may not have been expressly granted to the buyer. However, the law would support the conclusion that the right to use these facilities was implied by the very idea of the development being a planned community. As you can see, implied easements are subject to a good deal of interpretation.

Finally, the law of most states recognizes *prescriptive easements*. These involve the claim of right on the part of anyone who continuously and openly uses a path, beach, or other area for a certain period of time (such as five years). Any easement can be lost if a similar period of non-use occurs. Prescriptive easements will not be disclosed by a title search.

Lis Pendens

"Lis pendens" is the legal term for "suit pending" and refers to a recorded notice of a lawsuit, the outcome of which may affect title to a certain property. In a typical example, the unpaid holder of a mortgage on a property files a foreclosure suit against the property owner. As part of this process, the mortgage holder gives notice of a lis pendens so that all other interested parties are aware of the pending suit. This makes it just about impossible for the owner to sell the property, since most prospective buyers would make resolving the lawsuit a precondition of sale. Of course, an owner under this kind of pressure may be willing to sell a property at a highly discounted price.

Clouds Against Title

A cloud against title is a claim by another party or evidence that raises doubts about who is the rightful owner of a piece of property. Examples are:

- a family member contesting the validity of a will left by the deceased owner of the property

- a "break" in the chain of title, casting doubt on the current ownership (such as no recorded evidence of conveyance by Owner One to Owner Two, thus casting doubt on Owner Five's title to the property)

- a failure of a group of heirs to sign a deed properly when a property is sold at a probate sale

- claims of ownership of a portion of the property acquired by adverse possession

You or the landowner almost always have to remove any cloud on title before acquiring land or easements. After all, it would be folly to pay money for land only to find out that the person you bought it from wasn't the legal owner. In addition, you wouldn't be able to buy title insurance for the land.

If title can't be cleared (or the seller simply refuses to do it and a quitclaim deed, with which the seller transfers whatever interest he has without warranty or obligation, cannot be obtained), you will need to decide what risk the cloud poses. This is largely a legal inquiry. Only under exceptional circumstances should you take title subject to a cloud.

Quieting Title

When the Longtree Valley Land Conservation Society became serious about purchasing an historic cabin site from elderly Mrs. Rudnick, they ordered a title report through the local title company. What they saw was a mess. The ownership was reported to be in thirteen different people, as the result of the bequest of Mrs. Rudnick's father. "Oh, balderdash," Mrs. Rudnick protested, "that all was cleaned up years ago, I got the land and they got money under the will."

Well, further research failed to document any such deal. Further, it revealed that the deed to her grandfather had not been notarized, creating another cloud on title.

The society could not proceed any further with these title clouds. To clear up her state of title, Mrs. Rudnick initiated a "quiet title" action. Notice of the hearing was published, but no one showed up to challenge her claim to title. As a result, her title was cleared, and the transaction could proceed.

Outstanding Interests

An outstanding interest is the ownership right held by a third party. This outstanding interest may be joint ownership of the entire "bundle of rights" (a partial undivided interest) or ownership of some portion of the bundle, such as a timber right or water rights.

Mineral and timber rights. *Mineral rights* are the right to gain income from the mineral resources found in or on the land, such as oil, natural gas, gravel, or mineral ore. *Timber rights* are the right to gain income from any forest products found on the land. The owner of a property may exploit the rights for income, sell the rights to a third party, lease the rights, or sell the land but reserve the rights. Naturally, mineral and timber resources greatly impact the land's appraised value, depending on the nature and amount of the resource, extent of any previous extraction, ease of access, and market conditions for the resource.

Reservation of these rights presents a number of issues in a conservation transaction. Can the parties holding the rights build access roads and make "surface entry" to extract the resource? Should the party holding the rights be required to camouflage and clean-up the result of its activities?

You may not even be aware of what the mineral and/or timber issues might be regarding a certain property. Most title companies do not report on mineral and timber rights issues when they perform their preliminary title report, unless these rights are "of record," as they usually are for mineral rights.

In any case, your land trust needs to find out who owns or will own the rights and determine how the exercise of these rights might impact the conservation values of the property. If rights are reserved, your negotiations may focus on setting limits to those rights if possible.

A Case of Mineral Rights

You order a title report and discover that XYZ Mining Company purchased mineral rights on the land in the 1920s, something of which the landowner was totally unaware. What seemed to be a very simple and appealing project becomes more complex: you may need to locate and negotiate with the mining company if having the mineral rights is important to you. On the other hand, you might determine that it is highly unlikely the land ever will be mined. Perhaps your land trust can live with this small risk.

Water rights. Water rights can have a tremendous impact on land use and value, particularly in the arid West where water is a matter of economic life and death. The law varies from state to state, but generally there are two basic systems governing the allocation of water rights both above and below the ground surface. These are known as the riparian and appropriative systems of water rights.

Riparian rights are a legacy from the judicial tradition of old English common law. In this system, any landowner whose property is physically adjacent to the source of water has the right to use that water. *Appropriative rights* were created to adjudicate the limited supply of water in the West. This "prior appropriation rights" system was based on the old legal concept of "first in time is first in right." In this system, the first user of the water (sometimes referred to as the prior owner) is allowed to use all of the water reasonably needed to the exclusion of all others who might want to use water later. The appropriative owner does not necessarily have property that is physically adjacent to the water.

You need to know if there might be a problem with water rights. In particular, you need to know what the future conservation plans are for the land and whether there will be enough water to fulfill them, for which you will need the advice of experts. Consult your legal counsel early on when water becomes an issue.

Ways Outstanding Interests Can Affect Your Project

- Can you protect the resource without the outstanding ownership interest?

- Are there additional owners that you will have to include in your negotiations?

- If you intend to sell to a third party, such as a public agency, will this buyer accept the property with outstanding interests? (An agency probably won't.)

- How does the outstanding interest affect the land's value?

Partial Owner Complicates Negotiations

In your discussions with the landowner, you learn that the landowner's sister has a fractional interest in the property. The landowner claims that her sister doesn't want the land but admits that nothing legal has been done to eliminate the interest. You may be able to get the landowner to take care of the problem by requesting a quitclaim deed from her sister, or you may have to involve the sister in your negotiations.

Access

Having legal access is critical to any acquisition since land can be virtually useless without it. Uncertainty about access can affect your project in a variety of ways. For example, a title company usually won't insure for access unless access is substantiated by a survey. If there is any question, you will have to bring into your negotiations the issue of ordering a survey—particularly who will pay for it. Or if the access is over a neighbor's land, used for many years by the current owner in a friendly, oral understanding, the seller may have to prove access under law (such as by prescriptive easement) or get the neighbor to convey a legal access easement.

How to Protect Your Land Trust

All states have some kind of official system for recording and making publicly available deeds and documents affecting title. Theoretically, you should be able to examine these records to trace the "chain of title" backwards to make sure you're getting what you're paying for. In practice, however, title searching is complicated and in most places is handled by title companies or attorneys who routinely examine and report on title. This is the only way to develop a confident picture of the real state of title.

Title Report and Title Insurance: Your Protection

Title report. A title report is a document indicating the current state of title for a property, including the owner of record, easements, covenants, or liens affecting the property, as well as any defects or clouds on title. It is prepared by a title insurance company (or, in some states, by attorneys or title "abstractors"), which systematically investigates the state of title from such sources as the county recorder or similar agency, the county clerk, various tax agencies, the federal court clerk, and any other state or local agencies that might be involved in title matters according to local customs or laws. From this investigation, the title insurance company creates the title report, or abstract of title.

The title report is a summary of all the facts regarding title to a piece of land as they appear in the public records and as they are interpreted by the title company. In addition, it is the statement by the title company that it is willing to insure the existing state of title to the property, excluding any defects or clouds specifically listed in the report.

Title report nomenclature can be confusing. Title companies refer to the results of their title investigation as a "preliminary title report" (or sometimes as a "title commitment") because it is issued as a preliminary to, or as a commitment to, issuing a title insurance policy upon closing the sale.

Title insurance. The preliminary title report identifies any known existing "exceptions" to title, that is, any problems with or qualifications to the seller's ownership. However, this does not guarantee that there aren't unrecorded defects in the state of title that were not known to the title insurance company. Furthermore, the title report is valid only up to the date of its creation. Events subsequent to that date may cast new doubts on the state of title. The prospect of buying property the owner was not really entitled to sell still exists. That's where title insurance comes in.

Title insurance, which is available for both land and conservation easements, protects the holder from any loss sustained because of defects in the state of title other than those stated and specifically excluded from the policy. It is recommended that you get the insurance for transactions involving the purchase of land or conservation easements. Usually, in exchange for a one-time premium paid at the time of the transaction, the title insurance company will protect the buyer of the property against any losses incurred as a result of title defects for as long as he owns the property.

Ordering a Title Report

Getting a title report is almost always a good idea, but it can cost money. Order a report in the following circumstances:

- when your fee title or easement acquisition is a purchase, rather than a donation (if the transaction is a gift, get legal advice as to whether to get a title report and insurance)

- when you will invest substantial time and money in a project (in this case, it's best to get a title report early on in the project)

- whenever your site visit or negotiations indicate something that raises a red flag: you see something (such as equipment) that makes you wonder whether others have rights to the property; the landowner's description of past ownership makes you wonder whether there might be other outstanding interests; the land is adjacent to a body of water or railroad right-of-way (these properties are notorious for their title problems)

- when the land is to be reconveyed to a third party by warranty deed, by which you will have to warrant to the buyer the state of title

What kind of report you need varies by state and even region. Consult your attorney.

When do you order one? You do not necessarily need to order the title report before you sign an acquisition agreement. If you don't, you want to be sure the agreement includes provisions for ordering, reviewing, and responding to the title report and conditions that offer you an out if the title report reveals unacceptable state of title.

Paying for the report. The cost of title reports ranges from $250 to $2,000, depending on complexity. Sometimes (though not often) the reports can be free, since the company that completes the report will expect to sell the title insurance on the property. Updating an old report is generally less expensive than ordering an entirely new report; if you have an old report, ask the company that produced it to simply update it. When done in conjunction with the purchase of title insurance the cost of the search is often rolled into the cost of the insurance, which is typically based on the purchase price. Who pays for the title report and policy can be negotiated, although this is often subject to local custom.

Choosing a company. When pursuing title information, ask yourself whether the title company seems competent. Get recommendations from others. Find a company you trust and use it for all your projects (unless you are merely updating a somewhat dated title report, for which you should use the company that completed the original title report).

Reviewing and Responding to the Report

It is best for both the project manager and attorney to review the title report. Be sure to get copies of all documents referenced in the report, which are available from the title company.

When reviewing the report, consider any exceptions in light of the acquisition you are working on. If you intend to acquire the land, you have to decide whether the exceptions will compromise your ability to protect it; if you are working on a preacquisition, you have to decide whether the exceptions will be acceptable to the agency, something that can be hard to determine.

Exceptions you generally can live with include:

- common utility easements
- typical subdivision conditions, covenants, and restrictions
- access easements
- general and special county and local taxes not yet payable
- mineral rights with no access (these are sometimes okay)

Exceptions you may need to remove (though sometimes you can't):

- mineral reservations
- conditions, covenants, and restrictions that will adversely affect your protection plans
- water rights conveyed to a third party (depending on your project)

Exceptions that generally must be removed:

- mortgages (unless your land trust will assume the loan)
- judgment liens
- mechanics' liens
- notice of lis pendens
- clouds on title

Negotiating Language that Protects Your Land Trust

As described in Chapter 10, "Final Negotiations," your acquisition agreement spells out terms that will ensure clear title for you, the purchaser, as well as allowing your land trust the option of accepting the land with any title flaws. These terms include:

- title exceptions (what is acceptable and what must be removed by whom)
- title insurance (type of insurance—standard owner's coverage is usually best—and who is responsible for paying for it, something that may be established by local custom)
- type of deed used to convey the property

The agreement also may include a provision to adjust the purchase price to reflect the cost of remedying any title problems.

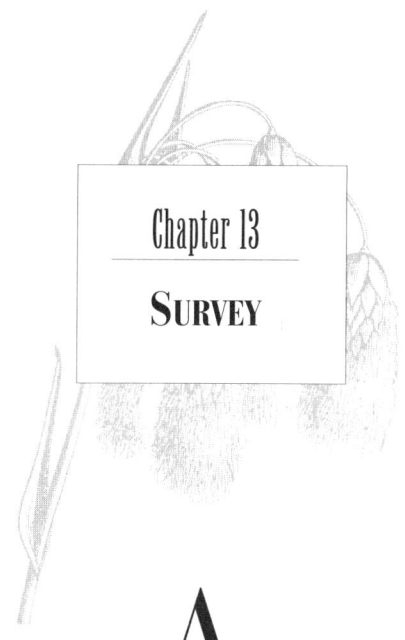

Chapter 13

SURVEY

A survey is a map showing the measurements, area, boundaries, and contours of a property. Just as a title report provides information about the land's ownership, a survey provides information about the land's physical features—information that can be extraordinarily useful in your negotiations, in your evaluation of the property for your intended uses, or as baseline data. If developing a portion of the property is part of your protection strategy, a survey is critical.

A survey includes:

- A narrative legal description of the property: This will be in the language of the metes and bounds descriptions (explained later in this chapter).

- A plat of the property: This is a plan or map of the specific area. The plat should include the boundary lines of the property and include distances, angles, landmarks, and improvements.

THE NEED FOR A SURVEY

The need for a survey can crop up in a variety of ways, as the following examples illustrate:

Acreage. You're about to sign an agreement with a landowner to preacquire a property. The purchase price is a fixed amount based on an assumed acreage. Before going ahead with the deal, you get a survey, which reveals a lower amount of acreage than you and the landowner thought. You renegotiate a lower price, in line with what the agency will be willing to pay for that amount of acreage.

Encroachments. Three weeks before the expiration of your option, you receive the survey you had ordered months ago when you became concerned about the proximity of a neighbor's outlying structures. Sure enough, the survey reveals that at some point the neighbor had extended his fence and moved a toolshed onto the property you are about to acquire. The landowner will have to negotiate with the neighbor to have the structures removed.

Access. A survey shows that the road from the highway to the property your land trust intends to acquire slightly crosses a neighbor's land. You find out from both the landowner and her neighbor that there is no formal easement, leaving legal access to the property in question. The simplest resolution will be for the current landowner to secure an access easement from her neighbor.

Dimension. You're designing a project in which you will sell off a single, already subdivided lot that lies adjacent to a public highway, while retaining the bulk of the property that includes the wetland your land trust wants to protect. To get the amount of money you need, the lot will need to be buildable— that is, conform to county zoning and building requirements. You're not sure the irregular shape of the lot will allow construction of a house consistent with setback requirements. A survey will help you make that determination.

Boundaries. The eastern boundary of a property you intend to acquire is described in the deed as "the middle of Old Man Creek." Rapid spring run-off after record-breaking winter snows shifted the creek to the far side of the floodplain, a good 500 yards from its former position. Depending on local law, this change in the natural boundary may or may not affect the property boundary (and the property's respective size and value). A survey should help you determine the location of the former and current property lines.

Location of easements. A property is subject to a pipeline easement for an above-ground pipe. The easement holder has not installed the pipe. You have a metes and bounds description of the course of the easement. What concerns you is whether the easement crosses the marsh, which is the main resource your land trust wants to protect. A survey will plot the location of the easement.

Presence of buildings, dumps, or other human-made features. The property you hope to acquire has a household dump that you recognize might contain hazardous wastes. A survey will show the exact location of the dump with respect to the property boundaries. Depending on its location, you might be able to offer to reduce the size of the parcel to be acquired by the land trust so that the landowner retains ownership of the dump site.

Confirming Boundaries and Locations

Do You Need a Survey?

Following are cases when you may not need a survey:

- You don't need to know the exact boundaries of the property (such as in a preacquisition of an in-holding in a national forest).

- A recent survey exists; this may or may not be recorded.

- The nature of the property or the system of describing land in the area (such as the straightforward township/range system, described later in this chapter) may make boundary determination easy.

108

- The agency you are working with on a preacquisition does not need one.

You may need a survey when:

- There is no survey of record (and you otherwise need one).

- Your site visit or discussions during negotiations lead you to suspect a problem, such as an encroachment on the land or a dispute as to the boundaries.

- The agency you are working with on a preacquisition requires one.

- You are concerned about the exact size or boundaries (for example, when your purchase price will be tied to exact acreage).

- The title issuer requires one as a condition to issuing an extended coverage policy.

- There are features on the property, such as wetlands, floodplains, or archaeological sites, that limit its development potential (and therefore may significantly affect its appraised value).

- Property to be placed under easement is not currently a separate legal parcel and you therefore need a precise legal description of that portion of the property.

Surveys vary in content from those that map only the property boundaries and do not show improvements to those that provide great topographical detail for development purposes. Their costs generally are proportionate to the level of detail. A perimeter survey, which locates boundary lines, may be adequate for open space acquisitions.

Managing the Process

Ordering a survey. Be cautious when ordering a survey. Seek recommendations for surveyors. Because there is such variation in cost, you should always get a quote or solicit bids from several surveyors.

Carefully consider timing: a number of factors can delay a survey. If the property is covered with five feet of snow, the surveyors can't work. If there are special features, such as a wetland, the survey company may need to detail a specialist to the task—and if this specialist is tied up on another project, you may simply have to wait. Establishing terms whereby you will pay the surveyor upon completion can provide an incentive to get the job done!

Briefing the surveyor. Be sure to speak to your surveyor early in the process and let him know of your interest in a survey that contains all of the following:

- measurements of distances within the highest established standards

- the kinds of specific information you are looking for on the relevant property

- any information about encroachments, protrusions, overlaps, and overhangs from an adjacent property that may impinge upon the surveyed real estate

- if applicable, all survey requirements for an ALTA (American Land Title Association) "extended coverage" policy of title insurance

- local zoning and setbacks, if you are asking the surveyor to survey a portion of the land for development

- text from the appropriate zoning ordinances

It's a good practice to accompany the surveyor in the field, at least on the first visit. You can point out special features, particularly those your land trust is interested in. You also want to be absolutely sure the surveyor is surveying the right property.

What to Look for in a Survey Report

When examining a survey report look for the following (unless it is only a perimeter survey):

- **Legal description.** The narrative legal description should match the survey map. Trace each course and distance on the survey, starting with the "point of beginning"; make sure the legal description "closes" and that it matches your understanding of the property's actual size and dimensions.

- **Access.** This should show any adjoining streets, roads, highways, alleys, and right-of-way lines, including their names, widths, and distances to the property.

- **Acreage.** Landowners commonly overestimate the amount of land they possess. The survey will establish the exact acreage.

- **Boundary lines of floodplain areas.** A floodplain area is a level land area subject to periodic flooding from a contiguous body of water. The survey should indicate whether all or part of the property falls under this description. The presence of a floodplain area will probably lower the value of the land, add to the expense of maintaining it due to increased premiums for flood insurance, and limit development.

- **Coordinate description.** This information should give you an exact location for the property in relation to its surroundings.

- **Corner monuments.** These monuments, if they exist, are important in that they physically mark, on the land itself, the exact boundaries of the property.

- **Descriptions of easements.** This refers to the location and dimensions of any easements that can be shown on the survey plat.

- **Roads, uses, utilities** not shown of record but visually apparent.

- **Encroachments and protrusions.** This refers to a building, part of a building, or an obstruction that physically intrudes upon or trespasses upon the property of another. Encroachments usually occur because the original surveys on two adjoining properties were faulty. A typical example is a building that lies mostly on the owner's land, but partly runs over the property line onto the neighbor's property. Encroachments can also refer to subsurface improvements, such as pipelines, that cross property lines.

- **Fences** marking the boundaries of the property or within the property.

- **Improvements.** This refers to any effort made by humans on raw land that adds to the land's value. Improvements can include buildings, streets, sewers, curbs, gutters, landscaping, grading, and the installation of utilities.

- **Utility lines** should include visible connecting lines to the property from public utility lines.

- **Surveyor's certificate.** This lets you know whether you are dealing with a professional with the requisite qualifications. (Checking qualifications is especially important when you are interpreting a report ordered and paid for by someone else.) Certification by the surveyor states that you are dealing with a true and correct survey, and should include the following language, or something similar:

  > "The undersigned certifies to (names of lender/borrower) (names of seller/buyer) (name of title company), as of the date of this plat of survey, that:
  >
  > This plat of survey correctly shows, on the basis of a field transit survey which meets the current "Minimum Standard Detail Requirement for Land Title Surveys" jointly established and adopted by the American Land Title Association and the American Congress of Surveyors and Mappers, the requirements for monumentation and surveys of the subdivision ordinance of the City of _____, and the current Amended Standards for land surveyors in _____ as adopted by the _____ State Board of Registration for Professional Surveyors and Land Surveyors...."

  The survey report should also include the surveyor's signature and seal or stamp with registration number.

DESCRIBING PROPERTY BOUNDARIES

There are three main methods of legally describing land: by metes and bounds description, by the U.S. government section and township system, and by recorded survey maps. Metes and bounds descriptions are very common in the eastern United States; in the West, the section and township system and the government survey system are more widely used.

Metes and Bounds Description

A metes and bounds description is a narrative that describes the property's boundaries, starting at a fixed point and following in detail from one point to another until the starting point is reached again. When you plot this description on a map, the result should be a complete, closed perimeter. This is known as "closing the description." Metes are measures of length, that is, inches, feet, yards, etc. Bounds describe the course or direction of the boundary lines, both natural and artificial, e.g., rivers, roads, trees, boulders, cracks, fences, iron pipes, and so forth.

The metes and bounds method is often used when there are no existing maps or surveys or when it is impractical to refer to the section and township system (see below). Older metes and bounds descriptions can sometimes be inaccurate or difficult to follow since they may refer to markers that have disappeared or been moved or altered. Such problems can render the whole description invalid. Even when technically accurate, a metes and bounds description can be lengthy and difficult to follow. If you are forced to rely on one, check it carefully by having a trained person walk the course described or plot it on a map (computer software exists that can do this) to make sure it is still accurate.

U.S. Government Section and Township System

The section and township system of describing land was created by the office of the Surveyor General of the United States in the nineteenth century as a means of identifying all public lands. It is based on a system of lines running east and west, and north and south, across the entire country. These lines form a giant system of squares that can be further subdivided into smaller and smaller portions.

The vocabulary for this system can be confusing. The lines running east and west are referred to as "base lines" or "township lines." The lines running north and south are known as "meridians" or "range lines." In this system, both base lines and meridians are six miles apart. The square enclosed by the intersection of two consecutive base lines with two consecutive meridians is a "township." Each township is subdivided into 36 "sections." Each section contains one square mile of land, or 640 acres. Each section is then subdivided into quarter-sections of 160 acres each. These can then be further subdivided into quarters of 40 acres each. Thus, the shaded area on the map of a hypothetical section 24 on the next page can be described as "the southwest quarter (SW 1/4) of the southeast quarter (SE 1/4) of section 24."

A reference system of "base points" exists to establish the location of specific townships. These base points are points of intersection for zero base lines and zero meridians; a number of these were established around the country and marked on topographical maps provided by the U.S. Geological Survey (USGS). A property can be located by first finding the closest base point. Then one can count the township and range lines from that point to find the specific township. Once inside the township, one can refer to the relevant sections and subsections to locate the property exactly.

```
2640 FT.
(160 rods)
(40 chains)

NW ¼          NE ¼
160 AC.

                  10
                  AC.

SW ¼          SW ¼         40 AC.
              NW ¼
              SE ¼

              SW ¼
              OF
              SE ¼
```

For example, in California, there are three base points: the Humboldt, Mt. Diablo, and San Bernadino base lines and meridians. Thus, a description might read, "township 16 north, range 6 east, Mt. Diablo base line and meridian" (abbreviated "M.D.B.&M."). From the Mt. Diablo base point, then, one would count up sixteen township lines north and six range lines east to find the relevant township on a map.

Recorded Survey Maps

The final method of describing land is by referring to a recorded survey map. These can take a number of forms:

- Subdivision Maps: Filed with the relevant state and local agency, these maps show the exact relationship of a new subdivision to other properties.

- County Assessor's Maps: These describe each parcel of land for the purpose of levying property taxes; in some states, assessor's maps do *not* provide the basis for adequate legal descriptions.

- Records of Survey: Many states require any surveyor who surveys a county property in conformance with land surveying practices to file a copy with the county surveyor; this is filed with the county recorder.

Multiple Descriptions

Actual properties, whose boundaries may be natural features, often do not follow the neat and clean division into townships, sections, and subsections. A property may cut across several subsections, sections, and even townships. Sometimes, to get the best possible description of a piece of property, a combination of methods will be used. The most common combination is to use a metes and bounds description to locate a highly irregular property within a section and township framework. In the Northeast, it is common to use a metes and bounds description together with reference to a survey map.

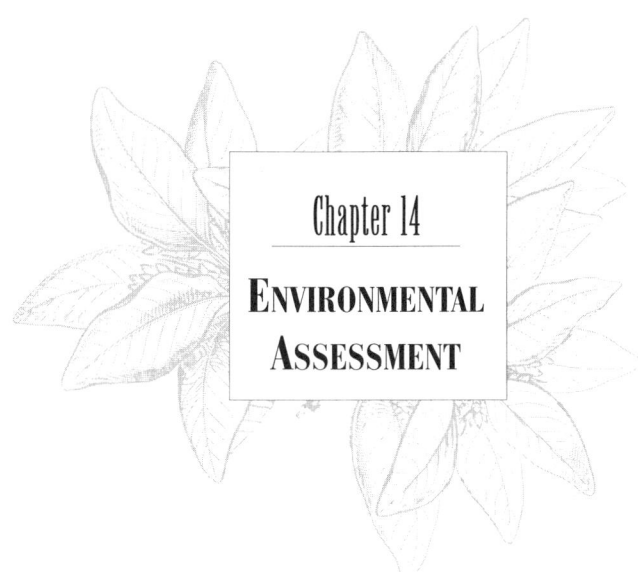

Chapter 14

ENVIRONMENTAL ASSESSMENT

Anyone who reads a newspaper or listens to the evening news is familiar with the dangers of land contaminated by hazardous materials. Cleanup costs can be very high; the property may be unsafe for public use; and the problem may expose the landowner to liability, regardless of who caused the contamination.

In general, contamination can result from:

- agricultural operations (such as the spraying or storing of pesticides), leaking fuel tanks, sheep dipping procedures, PCB-containing transformers, garbage or waste dumps, or contamination of ground water

- commercial operations, including chemical dumping or leakage or the presence of abandoned tanks or supplies

- mining and timber operations, especially chemicals used in processing

- residential buildings, especially those that contain asbestos

Federal and some state laws now impose "strict liability" (that is, liability regardless of fault) on current owners of polluted property, or on prior owners if the contamination occurred during their ownership. In other words, regardless of fault, anyone in the chain of title can be at severe risk for cleanup costs (and insurance against such liability generally is not available).

The most important goals of a land trust's policy on hazardous materials should be to:

- discover any problem before a decision is made to acquire land

- not acquire contaminated land (unless the resource value outweighs the hazards and the trust is prepared to assume the legal and financial risks of owning and cleaning up the property)

- complete all "due diligence" steps that will position the land trust to take advantage of any legal defenses available in the event a problem is discovered after the trust has taken title

LEGAL PROTECTION FROM LIABILITY

The law does provide some protection for the innocent purchaser of contaminated land. For example, under the federal "Superfund" legislation of 1980 (the Comprehensive Environmental Response, Compensation, and Liability Act, or CERCLA) and 1986 (the Superfund Amendments and Reauthorization Act, or SARA) any landowner who acquires land that already has been contaminated with a hazardous substance can escape liability if she is able to establish by "a preponderance of the evidence" that one of the following situations holds true:

- The land was acquired by inheritance or bequest.

- The landowner is a government entity that acquired the land through escheat or other involuntary transfer or acquisition, or through eminent domain authority.

- The landowner neither knew, nor had reason to know, at the time of the acquisition that hazardous substances had been disposed of on the property.

At first glance, it appears that the last of these is a perfect escape clause. However, it requires that the landowner show "due diligence" in examining a property for hazardous wastes prior to purchase. The landowner needs to be able to prove that she thoroughly examined the property, including having a professional site assessment, if appropriate, and found no problem. Unfortunately, there is not yet a clear delineation of what due diligence requires.

Steps your land trust needs to take. For every property your land trust acquires, you need to:

- assess the condition of the property and determine whether there possibly could be a contamination problem

- determine, if there is a problem, how bad it is and the nature and cost of cleaning it up

- clean up the problem, if required

- craft an acquisition agreement that protects your land trust from liability, whether or not there is a known problem

You must assess the property for environmental contamination before you close. This examination may be as simple as a careful, documented site inspection by a trained staff member or volunteer or it may be as complex as a full-blown professional environmental assessment, involving laboratory tests of soil and groundwater samples. If you are lucky—for example, if the property is remote, its history is known, and a trained person from your land trust has inspected it—you might be able to skip a formal environmental assessment. The level of investigation will vary, depending on the site and the requirements of state and federal laws. It is important that you work closely with your attorney at all stages of assessing the environmental health of a property and drafting your agreements. (See *The Standards and Practices Guidebook: An Operating Manual for Land Trusts*, Land Trust Alliance, 1993.)

First Defense: Looking for Clues

Your first step is to do as much investigation as you can in the early stages of a project, looking for indications of a problem or of a property's particular vulnerability to one. Ask the landowner:

- How and when was the property used in the past? Might this use have created toxic wastes?

- Were any fertilizers, chemicals, hazardous substances, or fuels handled or stored at the site?

- Are there now, or have there ever been, any underground storage tanks on the property?

- Are there any electrical transformers or capacitors on the property that may produce PCBs?

- Are there groundwater wells on the property?

- Is the groundwater in the immediate area used as a source of drinking water?

- Is the property the subject of environmental litigation or regulatory enforcement action?

- Were motor vehicles, machinery, or airplanes used in the operations conducted on the property? Was fuel stored on the property?

- Was any portion of the property used as a landing strip, storage facility, mixing facility, or for any activity related to pesticide application?

- Are there any adverse press reports or complaints on file regarding the property?

- Is the property near any floodplain, wetland, or other sensitive ecological area?

- Are there any improvements on the property? Has asbestos been used in these improvements?

- Is there evidence of waste disposal or landfill on the property?

- If the land was used to harvest timber, are there any sites at which chemicals may have been used to treat the logs?

- Is there any activity on adjacent or near-by land that might affect the property, such as a landfill whose leaching might contaminate the water source of the land in question?

To begin answering these questions, have someone inspect the property. It is essential that this person have appropriate training. While someone from the land trust should always walk any land the trust intends to buy, this usually will not be adequate for an environmental assessment, since some contamination may not be visible to an untrained inspector. The ideal is to have someone on your land trust's team who is trained to inspect land for contamination. In addition to noting problems, this site inspection should determine whether the suspected problem exists so close to a boundary that a survey needs to be ordered and whether there is any evidence (patches of dead vegetation, oil stains on the ground, evidence of illegal dumping, etc.) that a professional environmental assessment may be needed.

Document the site inspection: who has seen the land, how many times, and when. This documentation is crucial to meeting "due diligence" requirements.

There are a variety of additional ways to research the possibility of a problem, including:

- talking to the landowner (which you *always* should do), local residents, environmental organizations, or local citizen groups

- asking landowners of adjacent property whether they have obtained an environmental assessment of their property and whether you could review this (they may be unwilling to share it, particularly if there is a problem)

- consulting with university and other specialists (e.g., park planners, biologists)

- examining public agency studies and government records (such as records from the county recorder's office, county board of health, building departments, county/city planning departments, regional water quality boards)

- calling the state department of environmental protection for any reported incidents of contamination in the area

Negotiating an Acquisition Agreement that Protects You

As stated in Chapter 10, "Final Negotiations," a good acquisition contract should contain conditions that protect your land trust from liability and allocate to the seller the costs of inspection and remediation. These include:

- strong representation by the landowner regarding the existence of environmental contamination

- conditions on the sale under which the land trust can drop the project (and recoup its deposit) if the problems are unacceptable

- clear delineation of who will bear the costs of any environmental assessments and cleanup

- the landowner's agreement to indemnify the land trust if it incurs costs resulting from contamination

Because you often will draft your agreement before you know whether there is any environmental contamination, the clauses of your agreement will be broad. If the problem is known and analyzed at the time of the contract signing, the terms usually will be more specific to the identified problem.

Ordering a Professional Assessment

If you have any reason to be suspicious about a piece of property, consider ordering a professional environmental assessment. An assessment may cost you $1,500 to $10,000, depending on the size and nature of the parcel—which could preclude your taking on the project—but the risks of not doing the assessment could cost you far more; a major contamination problem could put a land trust out of business.

A critical step in the environmental assessment process is selecting, contracting with, instructing, supervising, and evaluating the environmental consultant. Real estate lawyers, title companies, agency staff, or experts on your land trust team should be able to recommend good consultants. Given current laws and regulations, environmental assessments are now as common as title reports or contractors' inspections. You should work closely with your legal counsel in all stages of contracting with environmental consultants.

What level of assessment do you need? The scope of an environmental assessment must be determined on a case-by-case basis. But as a minimum, the person conducting the assessment should take the following steps, which the industry considers a "Phase I" or "Level 1" assessment:

- inspect the entire property (and observe what you can on adjacent land)

- research the land use history of the property (and of adjacent land)

- search public records for evidence of problems

- document the steps taken and the findings

If the assessment turns up evidence of contamination, you will need to determine how bad it is. Work with an attorney to determine whether you should drop the project (either the resource will no longer meet the land trust's criteria or the potential liability could be too great), what further assessments may be needed, and the responsibilities of the seller under the acquisition agreement.

If your initial assessment identifies a problem, pursue additional information until you are satisfied that you and the consultant understand the nature of the contamination. You may decide to drop the project along the way any time you determine that the property is simply too contaminated or the landowner is unwilling (or not contractually obligated) to help with assessment or cleanup costs.

Phase II assessment and beyond. Particularly if there is evidence of a problem, you may need to go on to a Phase II assessment. A Phase II assessment, which can be quite expensive, consists of sampling and analysis:

- initial field sampling and analysis of surface and easily reached sub-surface soils to determine the presence or absence of contaminants generically and make specific recommendations for further sampling and analysis

- more extensive sampling through drilling at different levels and over a wider area (or establishing monitoring wells in groundwater) to determine the extent of the contamination, followed by laboratory chemical analysis to test for specific hazardous substances (some consultants refer to this as "Phase III" testing)

A Phase II assessment provides a much higher degree of certainty regarding the type and extent of contamination. It also provides a basis for estimating the cleanup costs. Phase III (or Phase IV, according to some) consists of remediation.

HANDLING PROBLEMS: CASE STUDIES

There are any number of contamination problems you might encounter in your projects. The severity of the problem for each of these can vary widely and is the key factor in determining how you proceed with your deal.

Household Dump

Your land trust has at last persuaded the cantankerous farmer to sell his 160-acre farm. In touring the property, you notice a smoldering dump behind the barn. The farmer explains that it's a household dump. Recalling something you heard at a recent land trust conclave, you ask whether it might have contaminants. The farmer is insulted. It's just ordinary garbage, he insists, "what you city folks have whisked away by garbage trucks." You back off the issue. Later that day, you and the farmer both sign the preprinted contract provided by the real estate broker. The contract requires the land trust to take the property "as is."

In the course of preparing to close, a neighbor of the farmer lets you know that there is reported "midnight dumping" of refuse in the farmer's dump, which is only thirty feet from the highway. You feel you have to look into this, and hire a local environmental consultant to look at the dump. The news is not good. There indeed has been unauthorized dumping of much refuse, including pesticide containers, paint products, and used motor oil.

The county agency for which you are preacquiring the property tells you that the dump will have to be removed and the soil proved to be clean. This costs the land trust $10,000. Ultimately, the property is deemed to be clean and the sale takes place, but the trust loses $10,000 on the deal and is forced to a position of fiscal crisis.

Household Dump Revisited: A Lesson Learned

Two years later, a ranch on the outskirts of town becomes available. You tour the property with the landowner and, again, this landowner shows you the "household dump," a site that was used to dump debris for 20 years. The owner swears up and down that nothing toxic was ever dumped there and no unauthorized dumping ever went on. Your instinct tells you that the landowner is probably correct on both counts. Nevertheless, having learned a hard lesson, you include fairly strong language in your agreement that calls for an environmental assessment to be paid for by the landowner and, should contamination be found, for the landowner to pay up to $2,000 in cleanup costs (the agreement can specify that if it costs more than this, the land trust can choose to pay the rest or walk from the deal).

The assessment finds no hazardous substances at the site and does not recommend further testing. It does recommend removal of the debris. Once the landowner removes the debris, you close on the deal.

Underground Tanks

The owner of a property believes there is no contamination on the property, and there is no evidence of any. You negotiate the right to conduct an environmental assessment at the owner's expense. To your dismay, the assessment reveals the presence of fuel tanks, abandoned by a prior owner, and the soil tests indicate that the tanks are leaking.

Your agreement specified that the landowner was obligated to clean up any contamination to a ceiling price of $10,000; if the cleanup would cost more, the landowner would have the right to terminate the deal. In fact, the cost of removing the tank and transporting the contaminated soil is $20,000. The landowner decides that it's worth it to pay the extra cost, since any other sophisticated buyer would require the same.

Industrial Waste

Your land trust wants to acquire a parcel for annexation to a county park. The property includes a building that formerly was a laboratory. The landowner discloses that activities on the site contaminated the groundwater, a situation that has been extensively studied by the company and state water quality officials. The owner believes that there is no continuing contamination and that the water will be cleaned up over time through a highly technical process known as "air stripping."

The land trust considers its options. After some study, the county decides it is willing to assume the risk of owning the property, but it wants indemnity from the owner. You negotiate with the landowner to indemnify both the land trust and subsequent owners against liability and fund the cleanup for ten years. You also get the landowner to secure this promise by providing a letter of credit for $500,000. To keep on the safe side, the land trust structures the deal so that the sale of the land is made directly to the county, keeping the land trust out of the chain of title.

Abandoned Mine

As one of its first projects ten years ago, your land trust bought a large tract of open land at a bargain price from a rancher who was sympathetic to your land trust's goals. The land trust did no environmental assessment. The land has been used for hiking and equestrian trails.

Seven years later, state officials notified the land trust that they had traced contamination of the creek to an abandoned mine site on the land trust's property. The state planned to clean up the site, the cost of which, under state law, would be the owner's responsibility, regardless of the owner's responsibility for the contamination. The land trust is stunned. Its attorney scrambles but finds no loophole. The trust's liability insurance excludes liability from environmental contamination. In addition, the land trust has no recourse to the prior owner, since the purchase contract required the land trust to accept the property "as is."

Two years later, the land trust is still mired in a lawsuit against the prior owner, but the odds are not good. The cost of the cleanup is likely to put the land trust out of business.

ACCEPTING RISKS OF ENVIRONMENTAL CONTAMINATION

Dealing with the risk of environmental contamination involves complicated legal and technical considerations and therefore is one of the most challenging facets of conservation land acquisitions. There are no easy formulas. Proceed carefully on each potential acquisition with the support of a team that includes an attorney familiar with the issues and preferably someone who understands the scientific nature of contamination. The most prudent and conservative advice would be to procure a professional site assessment on each property under consideration. Where acquisitions are going to be few and far between, and the cost is manageable, this is probably the right answer.

On the other hand, for land trusts that acquire multiple properties and have seasoned staff capable of conducting an assessment, it may be appropriate on occasion to forego a formal outside professional assessment.

Chapter 15
APPRAISALS

$\mathbf{A}$ppraisals are tools for evaluating the market value of a piece of property. They are a qualified professional's opinion of value, expressed in a formal document called an appraisal report.

Appraising is not an exact science, and working with and understanding appraisals can be bewildering. The appraisal industry is governed by guidelines, not rules; there is no one standard or format for reports, and what constitutes a "qualified" appraiser can often be difficult to determine. Appraisals should always be held open to critical scrutiny, analysis, and challenge.

Not all transactions require an appraisal, but if yours does, it's important that you know how to read and understand it, as well as how to order one, manage the process, and evaluate the finished appraisal for accuracy and thoroughness.

The focus of this discussion will be appraisals of open space parcels (or "vacant land," as the real estate community refers to them). Appraisals, however, can cover arrangements including easements, leases, and life estates. The principles articulated here apply to each of these situations.

ALTERNATIVES TO A FORMAL APPRAISAL REPORT

You may not need the detail supplied by an appraisal, particularly if you are not sure the project will ever reach completion. Consider the following alternatives to a formal appraisal report:

- **An "opinion letter."** This is a short written estimate of what a property may be worth, sometimes known as a "windshield" or "drive-by" appraisal. It is often used for fairly standard units of real estate, such as lots in a subdivision or certain types of timber acreage. It is usually solicited from an experienced appraiser who can create an estimate from experience and background knowledge without doing a great deal of research. It is not of much use for a property of any complexity, however.

- **A fully researched "value analysis."** The appraiser performs the research to reach a value conclusion, but does not write a complete appraisal report. Instead, she simply prepares a brief summary of the findings and briefs the client. Since approximately half the cost of an appraisal comes from writing the document and preparing relevant maps, this approach can give you a good idea of the value of the property while minimizing costs.

- **A "preliminary report."** This simply lists some comparables and sets forth a "range of values" for the property.

- **A phone call or meeting.** It is also sometimes possible to get the information usually contained in a preliminary report over the phone or in a meeting with an appraiser. This is sometimes referred to as an "oral estimation." It might involve hiring the appraiser by the hour.

Creating a Good Appraisal

Put simply, a good appraisal is a defensible opinion of value. It is not necessarily the best or the only opinion, but it can stand up to critical or legal scrutiny and can convince a skeptical reader that it represents a fair evaluation of the property. A good appraisal will be *complete*, containing all the background data necessary to arrive at a sound evaluation of a property, such as an estimate of value, objectives of the appraisal, factual data about the property, and limiting conditions. And it will be *logical and clear*—understandable to an involved, interested layperson. If after reading an appraisal you question where the value came from, you are dealing with a poor report. It is not enough that it prove to be accurate.

Considerations Prior to an Appraisal

Before you contract for an appraisal, you have to do some hard thinking about the exact nature and scope of the project. Inspect the property yourself and obtain a title report. Make sure you have a good idea of the answers to the following questions:

The process of creating a good appraisal usually includes these steps:

Defining the problem. The client and appraiser work together to define the nature and scope of the appraisal task and establish the terms of the contract.

- What exactly is your land trust buying? Is the acreage established?

- Will there be a reservation of use for some period of time?

- Is your land trust getting any or all of the relevant rights, including mineral, timber, water, fishing, oil and gas, etc.?

- Is there access or are there valid easements to provide access?

- Are there any title problems?

Collecting and analyzing data. Next, the appraiser collects and analyzes both general data, such as data about the region and the economic climate, and specific data about the property and other properties that will be used for comparison.

Applying approaches to value. Armed with all of this information, the appraiser applies the appropriate approaches to determining value. Traditional approaches are the sales comparison approach, income approach, and cost approach. Appraisers will also sometimes use a fourth approach: the discounted cash flow analysis. (These are described later in this chapter.)

The appraiser must decide which of these approaches are appropriate and which are completely inappropriate, and in some cases will use several.

Reconciling values. If the appraiser uses more than one approach, there may be two or three widely divergent estimates of value. The appraiser then determines:

- which method(s) seems most valid

- whether to rely primarily on the results of one method or split the difference between the two best methods

- which method(s) can be used as a "reality check" against the most valid method

The appraiser "reconciles" results of the evaluation methods by comparing these estimates and arriving at a final estimate.

Creating the report. As a final step, the appraiser compiles the appraisal report, capturing both the data collected and the thought process used to arrive at a value figure.

Key Concepts and Terms

An appraisal report is written in its own special language, with great weight given to certain concepts and terms.

Limiting conditions. A good appraisal report will contain a statement of any "limiting conditions" that underlie the appraiser's work. These are the ground rules for the appraisal, the assumptions that the appraiser is making. If any of these conditions is not valid or is subject to change, the appraisal itself is less reliable and may need to be modified, or in extreme cases is void. Typical limiting conditions include:

- The title to the property will be marketable.

- The legal description furnished to the appraiser is correct.

- The owner has title to the property and can convey it.

It is extremely important that you understand what these conditions are and how they may affect the value of the appraisal. Sometimes an appraiser may mistakenly assume a condition without looking into the issue in any depth, and the effect on value can be great. For example, it might be tempting to an appraiser to assume that a property can b⸱ ⸱ ⸱ ʰdivided when in fact it cannot. The appraisal should demonstrate wheth. ⸱ ⸱ ⸱ ⸱ ʱr under what circumstances the property can be subdivided, and the es. ⸱ ⸱ ⸱ ⸱te of value should be based accordingly.

Fair market value. One of the main objectives of an appraisal is to determine the "fair market value" of a given property or conservation easement. In general, property value can be defined by utility, scarcity, der⸱and, and transferability. It usually is seen by appraisers as an acceptable r⸱ ge of values, rather than as a specific dollar figure. The *Dictionary of Real Estate Appraisal* defines fair market value as the "highest price estimated in terms of money that the land would bring if exposed for sale in the open market, with reasonable time allowed in which to find a purchaser, buying with knowledge of all of the uses and purposes to which it was adapted and for which it was capable of being used." An appraiser, however, may set forth an alternative definition; make sure he clearly explains the reasoning behind the definition.

To estimate fair market value, an appraiser considers the property's physical characteristics—location, size, access, topography, and improvements—as well as any economic factors or social conditions that might affect the property's value.

Highest and best use. An appraiser's estimate of fair market value of a property is based on its "highest and best use," that is, a reasonably probable and legal use of the land that results in the highest value possible. This use must be:

- physically possible, depending on the property's size, shape, terrain, and access to utilities

- appropriately supported by zoning, restrictions, and environmental regulations

- financially feasible, that is, it produces a net income

If all three of these elements are not considered, the estimate of final value cannot be supported.

Approaches to Value

In general, when considering open space parcels, most appraisers will use the sales comparison approach as the exclusive method to evaluate value. They rarely, if ever, use the cost approach as a primary method, but it is sometimes used as a "check step" to validate the conclusions reached by the sales comparison approach or to factor in the value of minor improvements to the land. If an appraiser feels that cash can be generated by the exploitation of resources on the land itself, such as timber or mineral rights, she may use the income approach. Finally, the appraiser may use the depreciated cash flow analysis when there is a high probability that open land will be developed in the near future.

Sales comparison approach. The sales comparison approach (also referred to as the "market comparison" or "comparable sales" approach) involves analyzing value by looking at the prices of similar property recently sold. These sales are known in the trade as comparables, or "comps."

Because no two pieces of property are exactly alike, there is considerable room for error in the sales comparison approach. The art is in finding comparable sale properties and then factoring in how various elements of comparison might affect their sales prices. These "adjustments" to the comparables must be made in a persuasive and logical way.

The five most common elements of comparison in this approach are:

- *Financing terms.* Buyers may pay higher prices for property in order to obtain below market financing. The converse is also possible.

- *Conditions of sale.* These reflect motives of the buyer and seller, such as sale to related parties, sale under duress, unusual tax considerations, auction sales, or eminent domain. To find out this kind of information, the appraiser needs to verify details of a comparable property sale with at least one of the principals.

- *Date of sale.* Past sales must be considered in light of changes in market conditions. This is estimated by either a comparison of two sales of a comparable property over a period of time or paired comparison of two sales that are similar except for the time of sale.

- *Location.* Values can vary widely within an area or between areas.

- *Physical characteristics.* Characteristics such as slope, vegetation, views, and quietness can have a great bearing on value.

Income approach. The income approach derives value by converting the property's anticipated future income stream into one lump sum according to a specific formula. The property in question must generate income, and this approach is rarely employed for bare land, unless timber or mineral deposits are involved. Under this approach, you divide the annual net income for the property by a "capitalization rate" ("cap rate") to arrive at the "capitalized" value of the property. The capitalization rate, which is a reflection of how much return it is reasonable to expect on the investment of a fixed sum, can be derived mathematically by studying similar properties, or you can ask local experts. For example, if a property generates $20,000 a year in net rents (I) and the capitalization rate is 8 percent (R), the value (V) of the property is determined by the following formula: $I / R = V$ or $\$20,000 / .08 = \$250,000$.

Cost approach. The cost approach is based on the fair market value of the land itself plus the depreciated replacement costs of any improvements. Since this method is tied to replacement costs, it is rarely, if ever, used for open space. (In fact, because of the difficulty of estimating the replacement costs, this method is rarely used as the primary means of evaluating the worth of any property.)

Discounted cash flow analysis. The discounted cash flow analysis, or subdivision analysis, is applicable to property that can be developed and sold. Under this methodology, the future development value of a property is calculated and the likely costs of development are deducted. Next, a time discount is applied to the calculated net proceeds, adjusting this future profit to its worth in the present. In essence, this method will tell you what a developer should be willing to pay for a property given a potential profit down the road and, as such, it is similar to the income approach. This form of analysis is exceedingly difficult.

Appraising Easements

The key difference between a conservation easement appraisal and conventional appraisals lies in the methodology used to arrive at an estimate of value. Because each easement is unique and because easements rarely are bought or sold on the open market, their value usually cannot be directly calculated by looking at comparable sales. Instead, appraisers have developed a technique of indirect calculation, called the "before and after" method, to arrive at an approximate value. The appraiser estimates what the property was worth before the easement existed and what the property will be worth after the easement. The difference between the two represents the degree to which an easement changes the value of a piece of property. Obviously, the more restrictive the easement, the more it will reduce the value of the property. (See *Appraising Easements: Guidelines for the Valuation of Historic Preservation and Land Conservation Easements*, Land Trust Alliance and the National Trust for Historic Preservation, 1990.)

MANAGING THE APPRAISAL PROCESS

Who Should Pay for the Appraisal?

There may be several parties involved in a transaction who could pay for all or part of an appraisal. The landowner may be willing to pay part of the appraisal costs, particularly if she is not willing to proceed with negotiations without a firm idea of what the purchase price will be (and landowners tend to have more faith in the appraisal if they share the cost). In a preacquisition, a public agency may reimburse the land trust for part or all of the cost of an appraisal if it accepts the appraisal and closes the acquisition. (If a land trust pays for the appraisal of a donated property or conservation easement, this may turn the gift into a bargain sale, which will affect tax deductibility.)

With or without the possibility of reimbursement, there are several factors that could compel the land trust to pay for the appraisal:

Timing. If speed is essential in making the deal, be prepared to pay for the appraisal.

Confidentiality. If the land trust pays for the appraisal, the information is proprietary. If negotiations are delicate, and you wish to keep the appraisal information to yourself, be prepared to carry the cost. You may even wish to keep to yourself the fact that you have had an appraisal performed at all (but don't forget that a thorough appraisal will likely require consultation with the owner).

Pressures on the appraiser. Appraisers may tend to overestimate land values when working directly for a landowner and to underestimate values when working directly for an agency, neither of which may be in the best interest of the land trust. If the appraiser is working for someone other than the land trust, consider what slant this may give the appraisal.

The difficulty of the project. If a project presents difficult appraisal issues, you may want the highest quality—and possibly most expensive—appraisal. If the landowner or any agency you are working with wants to go with a less costly appraiser (some agencies, for example, are required to go with the lowest bidder for an appraisal), you may decide it's best to pay for the appraisal yourself.

Selecting an Appraiser

If you are ordering the appraisal, ask your sources—colleagues, public agency staff, bankers, realtors, attorneys, or professional associations—to recommend prospective appraisers. Look at client references, membership in professional associations, knowledge of local conditions, knowledge of type of land, availability and ability to work within your time frame, and, in the case of a preacquisition, the appraiser's acceptability to the public agency.

Briefing the Appraiser

Discuss the project with the appraiser you hire. (If your project is a preacquisition, it may help to have the appraiser also meet with and be briefed by the public agency reviewers.) Make sure that:

- The problem is defined and there are no differences of opinion about the work to be performed.

- The appraiser is aware of all deadlines.

- You agree on which documents and reports are to be provided to the appraiser.

- The appraiser doesn't have any misconceptions about the property.

- The appraiser is aware of any outstanding issues or concerns on the part of your land trust.

Briefing the appraiser can be a delicate matter. According to appraisal ethics, the appraiser is dedicated to determining the property's fair market value. Therefore, he should not be influenced by the needs of any of the participants in a transaction. In reality, however, appraisers are influenced by what they perceive to be your needs. It's important to discover any preconceptions the appraiser may have and how these may affect his evaluation of the property.

Moving the Process Along

Although an experienced appraiser will be able to do the work with a minimum of supervision, it is in your interest to ensure that the process moves forward smoothly by:

- providing information, such as surveys, preliminary title reports, specialized appraisals of timber and/or mineral rights

- making sure the appraiser meets any deadlines, such as preliminary draft of the final reports and oral briefings

- resolving any disputes between the appraiser and other involved parties, such as the original seller or the final purchasing agency

Get a copy of the report as soon as it is done. In fact, it is often a good idea to ask to see the rough draft of the report so that you can give the appraiser your questions and comments before he has gone too far.

Reviewing an Appraisal Ordered by Someone Else

If you receive an appraisal from the landowner or other party, determine whether you believe you can rely on it or need to commission your own by looking at the following:

- any potential bias shown by the appraiser

- the quality of the work (whether it is up to the standards required for the project)

- the date when the appraisal was actually performed (don't confuse this date with the date the appraisal was sent to you or "reviewed" by an appraiser)

REVIEWING AN APPRAISAL

Reviewing the appraisal report is critical. You will be deciding whether the appraiser has come up with a fair valuation and whether you need additional information or another meeting with the appraiser. Keys to successfully evaluating appraisals are (1) visiting the property yourself and (2) allowing plenty of time to read the appraisal from cover to cover.

As you gain experience reading appraisals, you will learn that there are some common red flags that signal a problem with the appraiser's work.

Who Actually Performed the Appraisal?

Check the cover page and any statement of qualifications carefully. Sometimes you will find that an "assistant appraiser" or an "associate appraiser"—not the qualified expert you engaged—actually visited the site and performed the crucial hands-on elements of the analysis. If you have any questions about the assistant's qualifications or work, call the most qualified appraiser who has signed the report and discuss the property. Make sure that she knows the property well, is comfortable with the conclusions and values reached, and has done more than simply sign her name to someone else's work.

A Flawed Appraisal

The St. Martins County Land Conservation Society had long sought to promote public ownership of coastal islands. Recently, the owner of a small island indicated interest in selling it to the society at its "market value." To indicate his understanding of the property's value, he forwarded an appraisal.

The society turned to a real estate attorney on their board of directors, who reviewed the appraisal and reported that it was deeply flawed. The appraisal had not taken into account the "sovereign lands doctrine," whereby certain tidal lands are deemed owned by the public. He estimated that the appraisal overstated the market value by as much as 50 percent.

The society commissioned its own appraisal. Based on a more realistic notion of value, the society and landowner reached agreement on a sale.

What Are the Limiting Conditions of the Appraisal?

The limiting conditions define the parameters of the appraiser's work. Scrutinize these conditions carefully to determine that:

- Your understanding of these conditions is the same as the appraiser's.

- The appraiser hasn't written in so many conditions that the entire appraisal is suspect.

- The appraiser has not made an unrealistic assumption that undercuts the entire appraisal. For example, consider a case where the appraisal assumes a subdivision permit will be granted although there is currently a building moratorium and a probable five-year delay. You may have to go back to the appraiser and request another evaluation of the property based on the likelihood of no subdivision.

Has the Appraiser Clearly Defined and Described the Property/Estate?

It's crucial that the appraiser consider only the subject property. If the property has not been clearly defined with appropriate maps or photographs, you run the risk of talking about two different pieces of land or including more or less land than the landowner has.

Make sure that the appraiser has indeed visited the site and taken a good look at it, has considered all of the physical factors that can affect the value, and has described in detail all of the physical improvements on the land. Also make sure that the appraiser has looked at the property not simply as a piece of land, but also as an "estate"; that is, as a totality including such varied items and issues as mineral reservations, tenancies, outstanding claims, life estates, and so on.

Has the Appraiser Adequately Described Access to the Property?

Ease of access can have a crucial effect on property values. The appraiser should consider the following questions:

- Is there adequate physical access to the property? This can include its distance from major communities, its distance from paved highways, and the type of road that runs up to the property line.

- Is there adequate access to all parts of the property (taking into account interior roads and natural obstacles)?

- Does legal access depend on an easement from another property owner?

- Are there any existing easements held by other parties that affect access to the property?

How Well Has the Appraiser Defined the "Highest and Best Use"?

Note the definition of highest and best use. All the resulting value estimates will flow from this, so make sure the appraiser has:

- Taken into account any laws, zoning requirements, or easements that would either restrict or render impossible the appraiser's definition of highest and best use. In addition, consider where the appraiser has assumed that future changes in the law will affect the fair market value.

- Been imaginative when considering how a piece of land might be developed.

- Been realistic about both the suitability of the property and the actual demand from potential buyers.

- Looked at relevant political considerations that will affect the property's development potential.

This is particularly important when the landowner has procured the appraisal and has presented a development scenario that is unrealistic.

Has the Appraiser Used the Approaches to Value in a Logical Way?

When analyzing the selected approaches to value, you are questioning the appraiser's reasoning powers and financial expertise. First, you should check whether the appraiser has discussed more than one approach for estimating value in the report. Next, you should ask yourself how competently the appraiser has used each of the approaches. (Because of its complexity and importance in land trust transactions, the sales comparison approach will be discussed separately below.)

Shrinking Expectations

The Manitou Trust is close to a deal on the Cross X Ranch. The landowner, Helms, is asking $4,000,000, arguing that the 400-acre property is subdividable into forty 10-acre lots. This sounds plausible to trust executive director Helen Ribera, particularly with the explosive development climate on the California coast. In fact, Helms has proffered to Helen an appraisal done by an appraiser hired by Helms that establishes a value of $6,000,000—substantially higher than the appraised value of $2,000,000 done by a federal land acquisition agency one year earlier.

Before making a final offer, however, Helen decides to visit the county planning office. There she learns that current zoning for the property would indeed allow for a 40-parcel subdivision, but that there are a number of conditions. One of them is proving that each parcel has an adequate household water supply from an underground source, since above-ground streams are dedicated for agricultural and wildlife use. Helen looks at the appraisal procured by the landowner and notes that the appraiser conveniently "assumed" that "adequate water supply exists."

Helen then stops by to visit an engineer who serves on an advisory committee to the land trust. He pulls out the maps for the property and looks at predictions of available underground water supply. By his best estimate, it is highly unlikely there is sufficient water there for substantial development. Drilling test wells would cost thousands of dollars and could take a year.

Armed with this information, Helen meets with the landowner and explains that her research leads her to question the subdivision approach to establishing value. She says the land trust could only make an offer based on its likely use, which is ranch land. She offers $2,000,000, in line with the federal appraisal.

For the *income approach,* make sure the appraiser tells you how he arrived at the monthly or projected income. Is it based on figures from the property or from comparable properties? How was the capitalization rate derived? Without a real sense of its accuracy, you can't tell if the annual income projection is realistic. Small changes in the cap rate can make a large difference in the value of the property. A good appraiser may take this into consideration and give you several scenarios regarding both the monthly income and cap rate.

For the *cost approach,* make sure the appraiser states how both the value of the land and the replacement value of any improvements were calculated. If these figures are not logical and clearly explained, the amount given may be a guess.

If you are dealing with an appraisal that uses the *discounted cash flow analysis* to appraise open space with a high development potential, find out: Has the appraiser adequately explained how the estimated revenue figure was calculated? How were development costs derived? If it seems like a fairly long-term deal, have inflation rates, both for land and costs, been derived and explained? Finally, how did the appraiser arrive at the discount rate and what supporting documentation is there for this figure?

How Well Does the Appraiser Use the Sales Comparison Approach?

As stated earlier, most appraisers will use the sales comparison approach to value unimproved land, making adjustments between the subject property and the comparable properties to reconcile their differences. The appraiser should explain whether the adjustments are being calculated as a lump sum, percentage, or dollar amount per square foot. Scrutinize the adjustment factors to make sure the appraiser has taken into consideration:

- any significant time interval between the comparable sale and the appraisal (particularly where real estate values are changing quickly)

- the motivation behind comparable sales transactions

- the relationship between the seller and buyer in each of the comparables

- the effect that financing terms may have had on a comparable's sales price

- similarities or differences in location, ease of access, highest and best use, physical characteristics of the land and any improvements, use restrictions, and economic or social climate

In addition, check whether comps have actually closed versus being under contract or based on offers. (If they did close, did substantial cash change hands? If so, the comps are more valid. A closing financed almost exclusively by the seller could indicate a speculative or market manipulative purchase.)

Be on guard for too many large adjustments. Most adjustments should be no more than 50 percent; if higher than this, you must question whether the sales being considered are valid comparisons.

Ideally, you also should get the sense that the property being appraised falls somewhere in the middle range of the comparable sales.

How Does the Appraiser Arrive at the Final Value?

Perhaps the ultimate red flag is a shaky explanation of the final value. To be convincing, the appraiser must tell you whether the final value is largely the result of one method or a compromise between two or three. If it is the latter, which methods carried the most weight and why? Which approaches did not factor seriously into his analysis? Which approaches were used as a check step? How was the compromise reached?

Section IV

PAYING FOR THE PROPERTY

This section discusses some of the financial aspects of a transaction. Chapter 16 covers loans to bridge the gap between when you pay the landowner and when an agency or your own fundraising efforts provide permanent funds. Chapter 17 provides a quick rundown of funding sources.

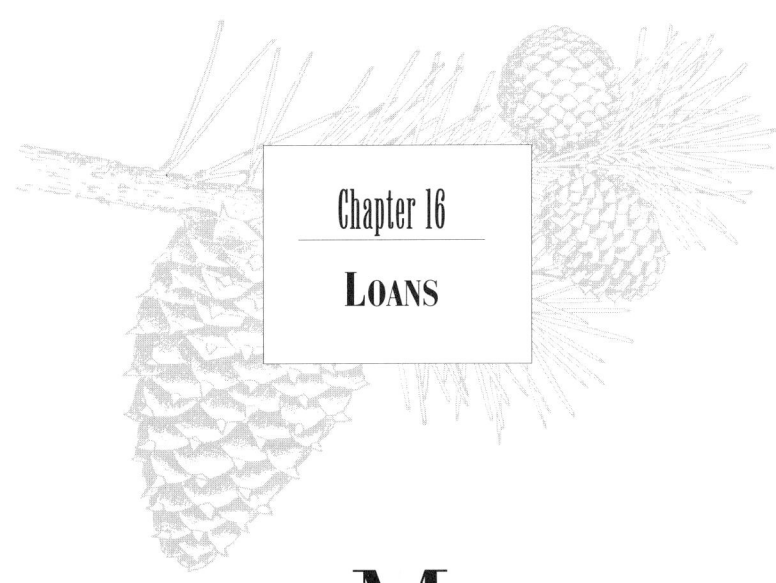

Chapter 16

LOANS

Many conservation acquisitions require financing to bridge the gap between the time you pay for the property and the time sufficient funds are available from a public agency or fundraising campaign. How you structure this financing is a key component of your project design.

HOW FINANCING WORKS

Financing can be provided by the seller or by a third party. Here's a typical financing arrangement: The seller requires a 20 percent down payment on the $100,000 purchase price for 100 acres. He wants the down payment to be paid immediately and is willing to finance the balance over a period of time. You believe your land trust will be able to raise the full purchase price through a fundraising campaign, but this will take up to three years.

To accomplish the deal, your land trust would be required to come up with $20,000 for the down payment and then to legally promise that it would pay off the balance of $80,000. As part of this promise you would put up some kind of security, or collateral, for the $80,000.

The seller would require a promissory note and, usually, a mortgage or deed of trust. The promissory note is the basic instrument of a financing arrangement. It is a legally enforceable IOU—a promise to pay a specified sum to a specified person under specified terms. In the case above it might state, "The Valley Land Trust promises to pay John Jones the sum of $80,000. This obligation bears interest at the rate of 9% per annum and shall be paid on the first and second anniversaries of this note. The principal balance and all unpaid interest shall be payable on the third anniversary of this note."

A mortgage or deed of trust is an instrument by which land (in most cases the property being sold) is put up as collateral to secure the promissory note. (Mortgages and deeds of trust are discussed in more depth later in this chapter.)

When Financing Is Inevitable

While you can avoid or delay the need for immediate financing by negotiating an option, there are times when financing is inevitable:

- A landowner in a financial bind may need a timely all-cash purchase. He is not likely to be interested in an option agreement or a seller-financed sale, unless his cash needs are limited.

- Sometimes a landowner must sell her land by a certain date, such as by year end. If you find out about the opportunity in late October, an option may not serve any real purpose, and a purchase-and-sale agreement with financing may be your only choice.

- A landowner may be looking for immediate property tax relief. An option will not meet the seller's needs—unless you can pay the property tax as option consideration.

- In some cases, such as an auction or another circumstance where there is competition from other buyers, the seller's terms of purchase may be non-negotiable. A fixed price may be due by a fixed date. This situation almost always requires outright acquisition. Since seller financing is not an option, other sources of financing must be sought.

Principle Elements of a Financing Arrangement

The terms of each loan are different, but they usually include the following.

Interest rate. Loan interest rates can be either fixed or variable in relation to an index such as the prime rate. It is usually best to negotiate a fixed interest rate that is as low as possible. Variable rates are more difficult to draft and administer. If you must accept a variable interest rate, take great care in defining the index on which the rate is based.

Repayment terms. Loans can be repaid in several ways:

- fully amortized, which means equal payments of both principal and interest

- equal payments of principal with declining interest payments

- equal payments of principal and interest until a given date when the outstanding balance is immediately due (a so-called "balloon payment")

Due date. The due date is the deadline for the final payment on the loan. Once the loan is repaid, the mortgage or deed of trust on the land is released by the lender. Try to negotiate a loan whose due date allows for delays in closing the acquisition or raising funds.

Prepayment rights. While the repayment schedule and due date set a time frame for repaying the loan, sometimes you will be in a position to pay off the

loan in advance. In your loan agreement and note, you may be able to negotiate the right to prepay a portion or all of the outstanding principal at any time
without charge or penalty. Some lenders, however, will not want prepayment
clauses or will seek to impose a prepayment penalty (preferring to have the
payments over a longer period perhaps to spread capital gains tax over time or
simply to have a steady income over time).

It is always best to try to negotiate prepayment rights, for several reasons:

- If interest rates fall, it may be in your financial interest to repay the loan.

- Not having prepayment rights can complicate reselling of the land, since
  the subsequent buyer may not want to acquire the land encumbered by a
  mortgage (most public agencies, for example, cannot accept mortgaged
  land).

- Negotiating prepayment rights at a later date can be difficult and
  expensive.

A negotiating tip: don't bring up prepayment in the early stages of negotiations. Hope for the best and insert prepayment terms in your draft agreement.
Lenders often are agreeable to the idea.

If you cannot get prepayment rights, negotiate a "substitution of security"
clause. This allows your land trust to substitute other security—such as a deed
of trust on another property or a letter of credit—for the original security provided in the loan agreement. Your repayment terms will remain as they were,
but you can release the property from the mortgage if you need to.

Form of security. Most lenders want their loans to be secured by some
form of collateral, usually by the land itself. Buyers generally try to give as little security as possible, while sellers want as much as possible.

A mortgage is a written instrument that creates a lien on a piece of real property as security for the payment of a debt. A deed of trust is functionally the
same as a mortgage, except that the "trustee" holds a deed to the property to
secure repayment. If there is a default, the trustee can sell the property in order
to pay off the loan. The mortgage or deed of trust serving as loan security may
be either on the property involved in the sale or on another property owned
by the borrower.

In a mortgage or deed of trust, you will want to negotiate a substitution of
security, as described above. In addition, you might negotiate a partial release
clause, which allows the owner of property subject to a mortgage or deed of
trust to pay off a portion of the loan in order to free a portion of the property
from the mortgage. You then can resell the released portion—for example, can
sell specific lots as part of a limited development. Without a partial release
clause, you would have to pay off the entire debt before acquiring the right to
sell off any part of the property.

From the lender's point of view, the payment for the release must be large
enough so that the unpaid portion of the note still is adequately secured by the
property remaining.

Subordination/Precedence among Lenders

Several loans may be taken out against a single piece of property. A key question in the case of multiple lenders is who takes precedence in the event of a foreclosure. This question is of particular concern in cases where the debtor defaults and the sale of the property does not raise enough money to pay off all the mortgages. In this case, the mortgages are paid off in order of their seniority. The instrument with priority will be known as the first deed of trust (or first mortgage); the next will be known as the second deed of trust (or second mortgage), and so forth.

A *letter of credit* from a financial institution is a promise by the bank to pay an obligation of its customer (the "account party") to the "beneficiary" if the account party defaults. If there is a default, the beneficiary notifies the lender, and payment is made.

A *loan guarantee* is a legally enforceable agreement by a third party to make payment on behalf of the borrower in case of default on a payment. A guarantee is useful when the borrower's credit is inadequate.

A *pledge of personal property* is an agreement under which the lender may claim specified personal property of the borrower if the borrower defaults.

Recourse/nonrecourse security. The promissory note for a loan specifies what recourse the lender has against the borrower in the case of a default. A typical "recourse" note will specify that if the borrower defaults and the loan security is insufficient to pay the lender, the lender can claim money from or attach the assets of the borrower. A "nonrecourse" note specifies that the lender can claim only the property (or other security, such as a letter of credit) that has been pledged as security.

For example, a buyer borrows $80,000 secured by a mortgage on the land to purchase the land and then defaults on the loan. With a nonrecourse loan, the lender can force a sale of the land. If the land is sold at auction and the lender receives $60,000, the lender has no other recourse for the missing $20,000. With a recourse loan, the lender can go after other assets held by the borrower to make up the missing $20,000.

Note that a loan cannot be nonrecourse if it is not secured. If the note is not secured, the borrower is personally liable for the obligation.

SOURCES OF SHORT-TERM FINANCING

A variety of sources outside your land trust can provide bridge loans (short-term loans until permanent funding is in place)—foundations, corporations, other nonprofit organizations, individuals, and conventional financing sources. Your land trust also can establish its own "revolving fund," from which it draws funds on an interim basis for option payments or interim financing.

Seller Financing

Sellers frequently will agree to finance a property's sale price rather than lose the deal. When a seller is not looking for immediate cash this arrangement can present tax and other financial advantages by spreading the payments and the seller's gain over time.

Tax Consequences of Seller Financing

Tax consequences to the seller in a seller-financed transaction can be complex. A portion of the payments made by the land trust as it repays the loan represents a tax-free return of capital, a portion represents capital gain taxable at capital gain rates, and a portion represents ordinary income taxable at ordinary income rates (currently, capital gains are taxed at a slightly lower rate than ordinary income). If the promissory note from the land trust to the seller bears no interest or bears interest that is below market rates, IRS regulations may require that the transaction be recharacterized to "impute" interest income. This means that a portion of the amount owed by the land trust would be attributed to interest, with a corresponding reduction in the stated purchase price. As a result, the seller would have to recognize greater interest income (but also would be able to take an off-setting deduction for the interest payment). The reduction in the purchase price would increase the charitable gift of value by the seller (the gift being the difference between the property's fair market value and the price paid by the land trust).

Advantages:

- The time and paperwork involved in obtaining seller financing are minimal compared to other methods.

- If the landowner can realize tax benefits from financing the sale, she may give you more favorable terms than could be obtained from other sources.

- Seller financing is generally easier to renegotiate than conventional financing.

Disadvantages:

- The seller's expectation of rate of interest is usually higher than that of a charitable lender, such as a foundation or friendly individual or corporation.

- When financing is advantageous for the seller, the seller may prohibit prepayment or require a prepayment penalty.

Buyer Financing

One often overlooked source of interim financing is the ultimate buyer of the property. This is particularly true where private buyers are involved, as in a land exchange or limited development project. In an exchange, you can ask the buyer to advance the money into escrow or make a loan to your land trust outside of escrow, which will be paid back at a later date by the conveyance of the property; in limited development projects, you frequently can line up presales. If you are preacquiring a property, some acquiring entities, such as some New England towns, can advance funds for interim acquisition when they have partial funding available for an acquisition.

Individuals/Corporations

An interested individual or corporation that strongly supports an acquisition effort can offer a loan to facilitate interim ownership. This allows the donor to contribute to a major conservation effort without permanently depleting charitable reserves. Individuals and corporations may be inclined to offer bridge financing because of conservation interests, the potential for beneficial publicity, personal interests (for example, to make a memorial designation), or indirect economic benefits (for example, because they own adjoining land).

Advantages:

- It is often possible to negotiate favorable terms.

- A charitably motivated donor may be willing to convert a loan into a grant or roll a loan over into another project.

- In the process of locating loans, you may develop contacts who will be sources of funding or financing for future projects.

Disadvantages:

- Available funds may be limited, necessitating more than one source of financing. (Many small loans can become an administrative headache, especially if they are all secured individually. Your counsel can draft a "master note and mortgage" whereby all lenders are pooled, similar to the way stockholders are.)

- The effort can be time consuming, without assurance of a pay-off.

Foundations/Nonprofit Organizations

Foundations and other nonprofit organizations are potential sources for low- or no-interest bridge financing. Foundations sometimes make program-related investments (PRIs), which are loans for programs in line with the charitable purposes of the foundation. Tax laws provide for and encourage such loans. These most frequently are made for affordable housing or community development purposes, but some have gone toward land conservation. The best source is foundations that have already supported your land trust.

Some nonprofit organizations may be willing to contribute their funds toward bridge financing for a project they are particularly anxious to see occur.

Advantages:

- Low- or no-interest loans may be available.

- Foundation and nonprofit sources tend to have larger amounts of money available than individuals and corporations.

- These are potential sources of funding for future projects.

- Many PRIs "revolve," providing funding for other purchases as projects are closed and the money is repaid into the accounts.

Disadvantages:

- Finding financing can be a time-consuming process with no pay-off.

- Bureaucracy and paperwork may be voluminous and time consuming.

- These may have unusual restrictions on use and stringent security requirements.

Conventional Financing

Although bridge financing from alternative sources is preferable, sometimes it is unavailable. If you need money for a short period of time only, loans from banks or savings and loans may work for you. You will need to figure a higher rate of interest into your overall project costs. Be aware that unless you have influential contacts or an existing relationship with the potential lending institution, arranging such a loan is not likely to be quick.

Advantages:

- The money is there.

Disadvantages:

- Interest rates will be higher than from other sources.

- There is little or no flexibility in negotiating payment terms or extensions.

- Typically, there are high up-front costs (e.g., application fee, points, appraisal fees, title insurance, legal counsel).

- The lending institution may have very demanding security requirements such as a high ratio of land value to loan amount.

- Often lending institutions will not consider such loans on undeveloped land.

- These can be slow to obtain.

Line of Credit

Your land trust may be able to develop a financial relationship with a bank and establish a line of credit, that is, preapproved money for unsecured loans. (Consider calling upon conservation-minded friends to guarantee the line of credit.) Because money borrowed through such a line of credit generally has a higher interest rate than conventional loans, it's best used in an emergency when you know that you can repay it quickly with a cheaper loan or with permanent funding. Once you're approved for a line of credit, it's fast money when you need it. On the other hand, it is more expensive money both because of the higher interest rates and the annual fee that generally must be paid to maintain the line.

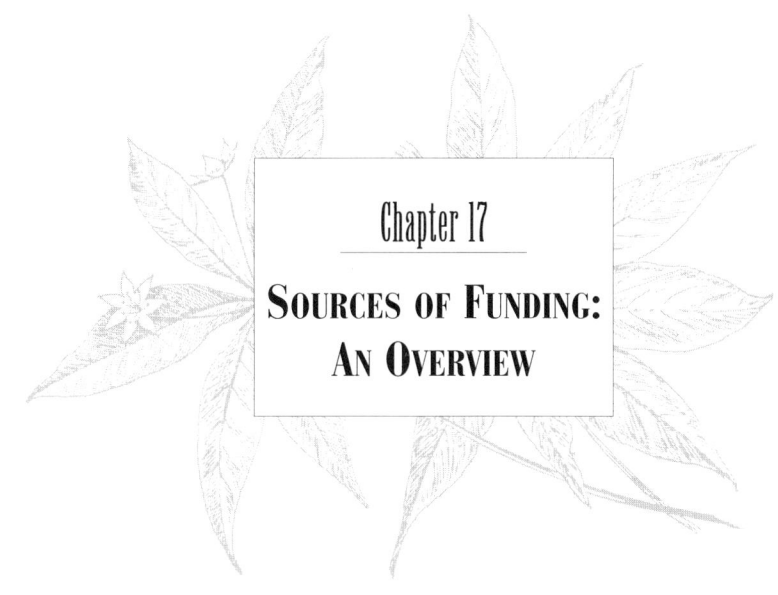

Chapter 17

SOURCES OF FUNDING: AN OVERVIEW

Financing can buy time and ease a cash crunch in an acquisition, but ultimately you need to come up with the money to buy the land. Land trusts draw upon a variety of sources, sometimes combining funds from several. This chapter presents an overview of the more common sources of acquisition funds.

BENEVOLENT FUNDERS

A corporation, foundation, or individual may be willing to provide partial or full funding for an acquisition.

Cultivating potential project funders is time-consuming, ongoing work, but essential for your land trust. The funder you talk to about this project may not come through until a future project, if at all. The amount of funds available from any one source will be limited. On the other hand, the process of obtaining funding can be quicker and less bureaucratic than with a public agency.

If you're looking to foundations, keep in mind that they may require lengthy proposals, and tend to disburse funds according to their own schedule, not based on project timing.

There are many resources available that list potential funders or describe how to cultivate funders and develop funding proposals. (The Foundation Center, with offices in several cities, is a good place to start. Call 800-424-9836.)

CONSERVATION BUYERS

A conservation-minded individual may be willing to pay a high price for a secluded or scenic natural area subject to restrictions. Usually a conservation buyer purchases a property from the land trust with the understanding that she will then give a conservation easement protecting its natural values to a land trust. (See "Conservation Buyer Programs," by Story Clark, *Exchange*, Winter 1989.)

Locating a conservation buyer can, however, be extremely time consuming, and such buyers often refuse to allow public access.

GRASSROOTS FUNDRAISING

Grassroots fundraising efforts can both raise money in the short run and build long-term community support. While these efforts generally do not raise enough funds to cover the total amount needed, they often draw the attention of major donors.

Combining Sources

For many years local citizens had used a small plot of ground (about 10,000 square feet) in the middle of Pineville for picnics, Christmas caroling, an annual festival, and so on. The plot had become known as Pineville Town Square.

The current owners of the land, who had purchased it two years earlier from the long-time owner, had received preliminary approval from the county planning commission to construct an office building. Local residents contacted the land trust to try to save the square. The trust approached the county for funds to buy the property, but the county said it didn't have the money.

The trust negotiated a thirty-day option for a consideration of $700. The landowners agreed to a $75,000 purchase price, the price they had paid for the property.

The trust joined with the Pineville Service Club and launched a "Buy a Square Inch of the Square" fundraising effort. The campaign, covered favorably in the press, prompted an outpouring of support from businesses and individuals. The group quickly raised $10,000. Meanwhile, they sought support from the Graniterock Construction Company, the area's major employer. The reception was initially lukewarm, but once Graniterock saw the degree of community interest, the company agreed to pledge $40,000 to be matched by citizens' contributions. When the pledge was announced, public support grew rapidly and a total of $35,400 was raised through the "square inch" campaign.

Based on the show of public support and the associated publicity, the county ultimately contributed $7,500 toward purchase of the property. This contribution brought the fundraising effort to a total of $42,900. The trust purchased the property, conveyed it to the county, and broke even.

STATE AND LOCAL FUNDING

Despite tight budgets and competing priorities, state and local governments continue to fund open space acquisition, viewing parks, recreation, and habitat as "green infrastructure" important to the quality of life and the economy. State and local governments draw upon a range of funding mechanisms, some discussed below. The particular mechanisms vary by state and locality, depending on state enabling legislation. (See Appendix A, "Conservation Tools and Strategies.")

Open Space Bonds

General obligation bond initiatives have been a mainstay of funding for open space acquisition at the state and local level. These always require approval by the legislature, voters, or both. General obligation bonds have the potential to provide large pots of money for land acquisition. In recent years, sizable bond measures for parks and open space have been successfully placed on the ballot in some states by citizen initiative. The initiative process, however, can be lengthy and exhausting, and usually there is competition for these public funds.

> Example: In 1988, California land trusts helped pass a $785 million statewide open space bond act. The initiative bond measure was orchestrated by a state umbrella conservation group that conceived of and drafted the legislation. Land trusts identified potential projects that were to be specified in the bond language, contributed funds for the campaign, helped gather signatures for the initiative to qualify, and mustered voter support for the referendum. The bond measure passed, and land trusts played a role in completing the preacquisitions specified in the measure.

Project-Specific Bonds

Some local governments can fund single acquisitions by putting a general obligation bond issue on the ballot or issuing revenue anticipation bonds. (An example of a revenue anticipation bond is when a city issues a bond in January to acquire an endangered property, knowing that the bonds will be paid back with property tax revenues due to come in later in the year.) Setting the wheels in motion for a project-specific bond initiative usually requires an opportunity that is compelling. If your land trust can negotiate an option on important land at a good enough bargain, it may provide the impetus a county or regional district needs.

Special Districts

A special district is a governmental agency that manages specific resources within defined boundaries. These can be established by local governments or by voter initiative, depending on state laws and regulations. Depending on its authority, a special district may be able to raise funds through taxes, user fees, or bonds.

147

Example: The Midpeninsula Regional Open Space District was established by voter initiative to preserve a greenbelt of open space surrounding several cities in Santa Clara and San Mateo counties in California. The mainstay of the district's funding is 1.6 percent of the property tax collected. While it cannot bond, the district has issued revenue anticipation notes and certificates of participation. The district has worked closely with the Peninsula Open Space Trust, a land trust that has arranged easements and completed preacquisitions with the district.

Benefit Assessment Districts

A benefit assessment district can provide funding for a small open space acquisition that benefits a limited constituency. Local governments can establish a special assessment district and sell tax-exempt bonds. Within the district, an additional sales or property tax is assessed to pay interest on and repay the principal of the bonds. Benefit assessment districts differ from special districts in that they are funding mechanisms, not governmental bodies, and do not have management responsibilities.

Example: Citizens of Fairfield, California, successfully challenged the city's annexation of three new subdivisions outside the town's jurisdictional boundary on the grounds that the action would cause the "premature" conversion of open space and agricultural land to urban uses. Under the resulting legal settlement, the city created a Mello-Roos Community Facilities District (named after the legislators who developed the state enabling language), composed of the new communities, as a way of financing additional open space acquisition. Each developed parcel is assessed an annual tax, which is deductible from federal income taxes. The Fairfield settlement also created the Solano County Farmlands and Open Space Foundation, a land trust, to direct the acquisition of open space with the proceeds of the parcel tax. Although the parcel tax has raised only about $300,000, the foundation has received additional monies from state and private sources in loans, commitments, and grants.

General Revenue Funds

Another source for open-space land acquisition is general revenue funds. Like the federal government, most state and local governments have a long and involved appropriation process. In state and local governments, an appropriation traditionally does not guarantee the expenditure of funds, since there are intervening bodies that must approve it.

Trust Funds

Several states have enacted trust funds to provide a sustainable principal that can generate regular interest payments for purchasing land. The strongest trusts are enacted by constitutional amendments that specify the use of the funds. Changes in these provisions require passage of another constitutional amendment. Revenues that have been used include: general appropriations (either one-time or ongoing), lotteries, mitigation funds, special taxes, and user fees. For example, Michigan funds a trust with oil and gas royalties; Colorado funds a trust through a percentage of the state's lottery proceeds. Trusts are difficult to establish and require considerable coalition and consensus-building to move beyond the proposal stage. When not constitutionally protected, they have been "raided" to cover budget shortfalls.

State Grants to Nonprofits

A number of states have enacted comprehensive programs that formalize a role for nonprofits in open space protection. Some state programs provide direct funding for nonprofits for acquisition and, in some cases, for planning and stewardship projects, either in a special nonprofit set-aside or in a funding category that both land trusts and governments share. Other programs do not provide direct project grants, but encourage nonprofit involvement in identifying projects.

FEDERAL FUNDING

Federal Land and Water Conservation Fund

The Land and Water Conservation Fund (LWCF) provides most of the acquisition funding available to the four federal land management agencies that land trusts typically might work with: the National Park Service, the Bureau of Land Management, the U.S. Fish and Wildlife Service, and the U.S. Forest Service. It also provides funds to state and local governments for park acquisition and development (although these funds have been severely limited in recent years).

Land trusts can benefit from these funding sources by selling land to public agencies funded by the LWCF. The size of the funding source allows for large-scale purchases. However, the federal acquisition process is complex and bureaucratic, and funding availability is never assured.

Other Federal Funds

In addition to LWCF monies, sources of federal land acquisition funds exist within some federal agencies. As is the case with the LWCF, these funds are available to federal agencies, and can supply the funding for purchases from land trusts.

Federal funding sources include:

- **Receipts Acts** (U.S. Forest Service). These acts, established in the 1930s and 1940s, allow use of a limited portion of the receipts from forest revenues for land acquisition by the Forest Service in the county of receipt. Funds are appropriated by Congress and any unspent balance for any forest in any given year reverts to the General Fund.

- **Sisk Act** (U.S. Forest Service). This act, established in 1967, provides a land acquisition funding source derived from U.S. Forest Service (USFS) transactions with non-federal public agencies. Essentially, the act allows non-federal public agencies to purchase surplus USFS lands. The funds gained from these sales then become available to finance USFS land acquisitions.

- **Migratory Bird Conservation Account** (U.S. Fish and Wildlife Service). Established in 1929, this account draws revenue from the sale of hunting stamps, day-use fees on refuges, and excise taxes on imported firearms. The account is administered by the Migratory Bird Conservation Commission, which allocates monies from the account to solve specific problems. Funds are allocated in several phases throughout the fiscal year.

- **ISTEA (Intermodal Surface Transportation Efficiency Act)**. Enacted in 1991, ISTEA provides federal funding for transportation enhancement activities including conservation and environmental purposes. ISTEA funding is available to nonprofits, private entities, private individuals, counties, cities, states, and other governmental entities.

OTHER SOURCES

Mitigation Funds

Some public agencies require a developer who is degrading a certain resource to provide monies to the agency or a conservation organization to fund acquisition of land with similar resource value for preservation or restoration. The concept is that developers can follow through on their original site plans, and the public agency or organization acquires a single manageable site rather than many scattered sites.

Depending on the program, a land trust may have a great deal of autonomy in the use of mitigation funds, or may be narrowly restricted to certain areas or types of land.

By definition, mitigation projects involve development of sensitive lands. A land trust should be extremely cautious about getting involved, scrutinizing a mitigation deal carefully to make sure it meets the land trust's conservation standards. Particularly if the transaction will result in the land trust having management responsibilities over a restoration site, adequate stewardship funds should be included.

Selling Remnant Parcels

Sometimes a property may be comprised of several parcels, not all of which are critical to your protection goal (or not all of which are of interest to the agency for which you are preacquiring the land). In these situations, your land trust may be in a position to sell off the remaining or "remnant" parcels to private buyers, allowing you to recoup costs not otherwise covered. The land trust should be sensitive to the desires and expectations of the public regarding the property and, particularly if the landowner sold the land in a bargain sale or in some other way made a donation, the land trust should make its plans for the property clear.

Limited Development

Rather than sell parcels that don't have conservation value, a land trust may subdivide and develop these portions of the land itself (usually working with a developer). This is a difficult and time-consuming undertaking, however, and can open up the land trust to accusations of developing land rather than preserving it.

Land Exchange

Federal public agencies own a great deal of land, some of which is less valuable or is difficult to manage. While public agencies are often barred from selling these parcels outright, they are free to exchange their excess holdings for more appropriate lands.

Many land exchanges require a third party, such as a land trust, to purchase the property the agency wants to acquire, to exchange it for property the agency already owns, and then to market the surplus land to recover transaction costs.

Exchanges bypass the uncertain and often tortuous road of legislative appropriation, but they are complex and subject to delays. An exchange may take anywhere from two to five years. As traditional funding sources dry up, however, land exchanges are becoming more important to the land management programs of most public agencies.

Briefly, this is how a federal land exchange works:

- The land trust identifies a private parcel that the public agency desires and options it.

- The land trust identifies a government-owned parcel that the agency will trade for the private parcel and finds a buyer for the government-owned parcel.

- The land trust exercises the option and acquires the private parcel. It then exchanges it for the government-owned parcel, which is sold to the identified buyer.

Appendix A

CONSERVATION TOOLS AND STRATEGIES

Rights and Interests in Land that Can Be Acquired

Right or Interest	Explanation	Advantages	Disadvantages
Fee simple ownership	Full title to land and all rights associated with land.	Owner has full control of land. Allows for permanent protection and public access.	Can be costly. Usually removes land from tax base. Ownership responsibility includes liability and maintenance.
Conservation easement / development rights	A partial interest in property transferred to an appropriate non-profit or governmental entity either by gift or purchase. As ownership changes, the land remains subject to the easement restrictions.	Less expensive than fee simple. Landowner retains ownership and property remains on tax rolls, often at a lower rate because of restricted use. Easement may allow for some development. Potential income and estate tax benefits from donation.	Public access may not be required. Easement must be enforced. Restricted use may lower resale value.
Fee simple / leaseback	Purchase of full title and leaseback to previous owner or other, subject to restrictions.	Allows for comprehensive preservation program of land banking. Income through leaseback. Liability and management responsibilities assigned to lessee.	May not be public access. Land must be appropriate for leaseback (e.g., agricultural).
Lease	Short or long-term rental of land.	Low cost for use of land. Landowner receives income and retains control of property.	Does not provide equity and affords only limited control of property. Temporary.
Undivided interest	Ownership is split between different owners, with each fractional interest extending over the whole parcel. Each owner has equal rights to entire property.	Prevents one owner from acting without the consent of the others.	Several landowners can complicate property management issues, especially payment of taxes.

Ways that Title Can Be Acquired

Technique	Explanation	Advantages	Disadvantages
Fair market value sale	Land is sold at its value at highest and best use.*	Highest sale income (cash inflow) to seller.	Can be expensive.
Bargain sale	Part donation / part sale—property is sold at less than fair market value.*	Tax benefits to seller since difference between fair market value and sale price is considered a charitable contribution. Smaller capital gains tax.	Seller must be willing to sell at less than fair market value. Can be expensive.
Outright donation	A donation by landowner of all interest in property.*	Allows for permanent protection without direct public expenditure. Tax benefits to seller since property's fair market value is considered a charitable contribution.	Ownership responsibility includes liability and maintenance.
Bequest	Landowner retains ownership until death.*	Management responsibility usually deferred until donor's death.	Date of acquisition is uncertain. Donor does not benefit from income tax deductions. Landowner can change will.
Donation with reserved life estate	Landowner donates during lifetime but has lifetime use.	Landowner retains use but receives tax benefits from donation.	Date of acquisition is uncertain.
Land exchange	Exchange of developable land for land with high conservation value.	Low-cost technique if trade parcel is donated. Reduces capital gains tax for original owner of protected land.	Properties must be of comparable value. Complicated and time-consuming.
Eminent domain (government)	The right of the government to take private property for public purpose upon payment of just compensation.	Provides government with a tool to acquire desired properties if other acquisition techniques are not workable.	High acquisition costs. Can result in speculation on target properties. Potentially expensive and time-consuming litigation.
Tax foreclosure (government)	Government acquires land by tax payment default.	Limited expenditure. Land might not be appropriate for public open space, but can be sold to provide funds for open space acquisition.	Cumbersome process.

154

Technique	Explanation	Advantages	Disadvantages
Agency transfer (government)	Certain government agencies may have surplus property inappropriate for their needs that could be transferred to a parks agency for park use.	Limited expenditure.	Surplus property available may not be appropriate for park use or the owning agency may want to sell to a private party to generate revenues.
Restricted auction (nonprofit)	Government restricts the future use of property to open space, then sells.	Property sold to highest bidder but restriction lowers price and competition.	It may be difficult for a nonprofit to convince government that a restriction will serve to benefit the general public. Can be expensive.

*Conservation easements also can be acquired by these means.

Management and Ownership Options Following Purchase by Nonprofit Organization

Technique	Explanation	Advantages	Disadvantages
Conveyance to public agency	Nonprofit acquires and holds land until public agency is able to purchase.	A nonprofit can enter the real estate market more easily than government, and can often facilitate a sale when the government agency would be unable.	Must have a public agency willing and able to buy within a reasonable time frame.
Conveyance to another nonprofit.	Nonprofit acquires and holds land until another nonprofit has been established or is able to finance acquisition.	Allows immediate acquisition even though acquiring group cannot or is not willing to hold property.	Requires existence or establishment of ultimate land holder that has solid support, funding and the ability to manage land.
Management by nonprofit	Nonprofit retains ownership and assumes management responsibilities.	Ownership remains within the community; local citizens can provide responsible care and management.	Land must fit criteria of acquiring organization. Organization must assume long-term management responsibilities and costs.
Saleback or leaseback	Nonprofit purchases property, limits future development through restrictive easements or covenants, and resells or leases back part or all of property. May involve subdivision of property.	Acquisition is financed by resale or leaseback. Resale at less than fair market value (because of restrictions) makes land affordable for buyer. Sale can finance preservation of part of site.	Complex negotiations. A leaseback means the nonprofit retains responsibility for the land.

Financing Options for Government

Financing Option	Explanation	Advantages	Disadvantages
General fund appropriation	Appropriation from general state or local government fund.	Avoids interest and debt service cost.	Budget allocations unpredictable. Might not provide sufficient funds, and competes with other programs.
Bond act	Borrowing money through issuance of bonds—a common way to provide funds for open space. Usually approved through local or statewide referendum.	Allows for immediate purchase of open space. Distributes cost of acquisition.	Requires approval of general public. Can be expensive—interest charges are tacked on to cost of project.
Land and Water Conservation Fund	Federal funds provided to local governments on a 50-50 matching basis for acquisition and development of outdoor recreation areas.	Cost of acquisition for local government is lowered by subsidy.	Depends on federal approval. Limited funds available.
State grant / low interest loans	States provide matching grants or low interest loans for municipalities to acquire open space.	Encourages localities to preserve open space by leveraging local funds. Donated lands may be used as a match.	Localities must compete for limited funds and be able to match state funds.
Real estate transfer tax	Acquisition funds obtained from a tax on property transfers. Percentage and amount exempted varies with locality.	Growth creates a substantial fund for open space acquisition. Enables local communities to generate their own funds for open space protection.	Places greater burden on new residents than on existing residents. Can inflate real estate values. Effective only in growth situations.
Land gains tax	Capital gains tax on sale or exchange of undeveloped land held for a short period of time. Tax rate varies depending on holding period.	Discourages speculative development. Has a regulatory and revenue impact.	Can inflate real estate values and slow market.

Financing Option	Explanation	Advantages	Disadvantages
Payment in lieu of dedication	Local government requires developers to pay an impact fee to a municipal trust fund for open space acquisitions.	New construction pays for its impact on open space.	Acquisition funds depend on development. May be lack of accountability for funds. Legality of method depends on relationship of open space to new development.
Special assessment district	Special tax district for area benefitted by an open space project.	Users finance acquisition and management.	Increases taxes. Timely and costly to implement.
Tax return check off	On state income tax forms, a filer may appropriate a small amount of taxes owed toward revenues for natural lands acquisitions.	Convenient and successful means of generating funds.	Vulnerable to competition from other worthwhile programs.
Other funds / taxes	Taxes on cigarettes, sales, gasoline, and natural resource exploitation; revenue from fees and licenses for boat, off-road vehicle, and snowmobile use, park entry, hunting, etc.	Income from fees and licenses pays for resources.	Revenues from taxes can be diverted for other uses unless dedicated to open space. Fees create pressures for money to be spent on special interest uses.
Sale or transfer of tax default property	Sale of tax default property can provide a fund for open space acquisition. Also, if site meets criteria, it can be transferred to appropriate agency for park use.	Funds for acquisition are acquired with little cost to taxpayers.	Need to assure that sale proceeds are specially allocated to open space acquisition. Might not provide a significant income. Very political process.

Financing Options for Nonprofits

Financing Option	Explanation	Advantages	Disadvantages
Loan from institutional lender	Conventional loan from bank or savings and loan.	Less time-consuming process than fundraising.	Long-term financial commitment for nonprofit. Higher interest costs than owner financing. Mortgage lien.
Installment sale	Buyer pays for property over time.	If seller-financed, can lower taxes for seller. Buyer can negotiate better sale terms (lower interest rates).	Long-term financial commitment for nonprofit. Mortgage lien.
Fundraising	No- or low-interest loans are acquired through program-related investments from foundations, non-standard investments from corporations, or charitable creditors (community members).	Community fundraising creates publicity and support.	A long, uncertain, and time-consuming process.
Revolving fund / loans or grants	A public or private organization makes grants to localities or nonprofits for land acquisition based on a project's revenue-generating potential.	Encourages projects with revenue-generating potential.	Projects with low revenue-generating potential have lower priority.
Partial development / saleback or lease	Nonprofit purchases property, limits future development through restrictive covenants, and resells or leases back part or all of property.	Acquisition is financed by resale or leaseback. Sale can finance preservation of part of site.	Complex negotiations. If leaseback, nonprofit retains responsibility for land. Finding buyer for restricted property may be difficult, and land value will be lowered by restrictions.

Government Financial Incentives for Conservation

Incentive	Explanation	Advantages	Disadvantages
Preferential assessment	Under state laws, agricultural and forest districts can be established to assess land as farmland or forestland rather than at its "highest and best use."	Promotes resource conservation and management. Especially benefits landowners in areas with development pressure. Tax base loss can be partially reclaimed through penalty tax on landowners who terminate enrollment.	Voluntary participation. Does not provide long-term protection. Minimum acreage for entry. Strength of program depends on penalty from withdrawals. Local government bears burden of reduced tax base.
Purchase of development rights (PDR)	Local or state government purchases development rights to maintain land in farm use.	Landowner can derive income from selling development rights and continue to own land. Lower property value should reduce property taxes.	Can be costly, particularly in a community with high real estate values.
Land conservation grants	State programs pay or otherwise enable landowners to preserve land, enhance wildlife, and provide public access.	Landowners derive revenues from preserving land without selling interests in land.	Preservation of land or provision of public access requires public expenditures.

Regulatory Techniques—Growth Control

Technique	Explanation	Advantages	Disadvantages
Phased growth	Permits a limited amount of growth each year.	Effective as a comprehensive planning strategy.	There must be an equitable system to approve development. Future development pressures difficult to predict.
Moratorium	Legal postponement or delay of land development.	Useful as an interim measure during the formulation of a master development plan.	Provides only a temporary solution and can create a rush on land development prior to taking effect.
Transfer of development rights (TDR)	An owner of publicly designated land can sell development rights to other landowners whose property can support increased density.	Cost of preservation absorbed by property owner who purchases development rights.	Difficult to implement. Preservation and receiving areas must be identified.

Regulatory Techniques—Zoning and Subdivision Provisions

Technique	Explanation	Advantages	Disadvantages
Large lot zoning	Large minimum-lot sizes restrict the density of development.	An established land use control used as part of a comprehensive plan. Effective at maintaining low densities and protecting water resources, particularly in rural areas.	Since zoning is subject to change, not effective for permanent preservation. Can increase real estate values and infrastructure costs and can foster urban sprawl.
Performance zoning	A zone is defined by a list of permitted impacts (based on natural resource data and design guidelines) as opposed to permitted uses.	Directs development to appropriate places based on a comprehensive, environmentally based plan. Can be implemented through cluster development.	Difficulties in implementation since environmental impacts can be hard to measure and criteria are hard to establish. Plan can be expensive to prepare.
Carrying capacity zoning	Based on the ability of an area to accommodate growth and development within the limits defined by existing infrastructure and natural resource capabilities. Often called Current Planning Capacity.	Zoning is based on an area's physical capacity to accommodate development. Can be implemented through cluster development.	Requires a comprehensive environmental inventory for implementation. Determining carrying capacity can be a difficult process, subject to differing opinions, quality-of-life assumptions, and changing technologies.
Cluster zoning / planned unit development (PUD)	Maintains regular zoning's ratio of housing units to acreage but permits clustered development through undersized lots, thus allowing for open space preservation. A PUD provision allows clustering for a large, mixed-use development.	Flexibility in siting allows preservation of open space areas within development site. Can reduce construction and infrastructure costs.	Open space often preserved in small separate pieces, not necessarily linked to a comprehensive open space system. May increase processing time for development approval. Lack of infrastructure can inhibit use of technique.

Technique	Explanation	Advantages	Disadvantages
Preservation overlay zoning	At discretion of municipality, overlay zones with development restrictions can be established to protect agricultural and natural areas, scenic views, and historic neighborhoods.	Special zones have regulations specific to the needs of a unique area and may be subject to mandatory clustering, performance standards, special permits, and site plan and architectural review.	Language in special district ordinance must be specific enough to avoid varying interpretations.
Exaction	As a condition of obtaining subdivision approval, local government requires developers to pay a fee or dedicate land to a municipal trust fund for open space. Also, states can require open space set-asides as part of environmental review.	New construction pays for its impact on open space.	Acquisition funds dependent on residential development. Commercial development often not subject to exaction fees. Difficult to calculate developer's fair share of costs.
Conservation density subdivisions	Permit developers an option of building roads to less expensive specifications in exchange for permanent restrictions in number of units built. Roads can be public or private.	Increases open space and reduces traffic. Discourages higher densities to pay for the higher cost of road building.	Requires enforcement of easements. Private roads limit public access and require homeowner association maintenance.

This appendix is adapted from *Tools and Strategies: Protecting the Landscape and Shaping Growth*, 1990, the Regional Plan Association, New York.

161

Appendix B

PROJECT TASKS CHECKLIST

Project:						
ACTION	**ACQUISITION**			**CONVEYANCE**		
	Responsible Party	Target Completed	Status/ Comments	Responsible Party	Target Completed	Status/ Comments
Contact owner						
Present term sheet/offer letter to owner						
Order appraisal						
Order title report						
Investigate water, mineral rights, tenancies, access						
Review title report						
Obtain leases, etc., from landowner, review						
Confirm title, timing with public agency						
Provide landowner with copy of agreement						
Review agreement with landowner						
Obtain signatures on agreement						
Mark relevant dates on calendar						
Pay seller option consideration						
Record memorandum of option						

ACTION	ACQUISITION			CONVEYANCE		
	Responsible Party	Target Completed	Status/ Comments	Responsible Party	Target Completed	Status/ Comments
Initiate environmental review						
Approve environmental report						
Exercise option						
Open escrow						
Prepare escrow instructions						
Prepare deed, etc.						
Review preliminary closing statement						
Close escrow						
Review and distribute final closing statement						
Prepare closing file						
Receive and file original recorded deeds, etc.						
Receive and file title policy						
Note due dates, amounts for any tenants, leases						
Apply for property tax exemption, if applicable						
Pay property taxes as due						
Prepare management plan for property						
Obtain insurance on property, if applicable						

Appendix C

PROJECT COSTS CHECKLIST

Project Name:
Date:
By:

Pre-Closing Expenses

Option/Purchase Contract
Option price / contract down payment $_____
Date option expires   _____
Date closing scheduled   _____

Preliminary Title Report and Advice $_____

Appraisal $_____

Expert Services
Attorney $_____
Accountants $_____
Hazardous waste assessment $_____
Boundary / subdivision survey (or land survey) $_____
Other consultants $_____

Direct Pre-Closing Expenses
Telephone and postage $_____
Travel $_____
Meals and lodging $_____
Photocopies $_____
Proposals $_____

Other
_____ $_____
_____ $_____

Estimated Staff Time
Direct hours   _____
Dollars for direct hours $_____
Overhead estimate $_____

Closing Costs

Payments in Closing
Options / down payments creditable to purchase $_____
Additional cash payments to seller $_____
Other:_____ $_____

164

Note to Seller—Note Terms

Face amount $_____

Due date   _____

Interest rate   _____

Periodic payments required

  Frequency   _____

  Principal $_____

  Interest $_____

Other:_____ $_____

Note to Seller—Security

Describe:

_____

_____

_____

_____

Note to Lender—Note Terms

Face amount $_____

Due date   _____

Interest rate   _____

Periodic payments required

  Frequency   _____

  Principal $_____

  Interest $_____

Other:_____ $_____

Note to Lender—Security

Describe:

_____

_____

_____

_____

Property Taxes

Full cash assessment $_____

Annual property taxes currently levied $_____

Prorated amount due on closing $_____

Tax period covered   _____ to _____

When next installment due? _____

Can exemption be obtained? (critical) _____yes _____no

If yes, when effective?   _____

Tax penalty due $_____

Assessments

Nature of bonded indebtedness (assessments)
outstanding on property:

_____

_____

_____

How and when principal and interest payable:

_____

_____

_____

_____

Current principal outstanding $_____

Current interest rate   _____

Years remaining to retire principal   _____

Amount required to retire indebtedness early (include

any prepayment penalty and describe procedure): $_____

_____

_____

_____

_____

Could governmental entity assume indebtedness? _____yes _____no

Title Insurance

Type of policy   _____

Amount to be insured $_____

Estimated premium $_____

Miscellaneous Closing Costs

Transfer tax stamps $_____

Escrow fees $_____

Reconveyance fees $_____

Recording fees $_____

Notarial fees $_____

Other:_____ $_____

Insurance

Hazard or liability insurance required?   _____yes _____no

Insurance company   _____

Policy amount $_____

Annual premium $_____

Expiration date   _____

Estimated Staff Time

Direct hours   _____

Dollars for direct hours $_____

Overhead estimate $_____

<u>Holding Costs</u>
<u>(Long-Term or Interim)</u>

Holding Arrangement

Length of time to be held   _____

How to be monitored/managed:

_____

_____

166

_____
_____

Plans for public access:

_____
_____
_____
_____

Direct Monitoring Costs
Baseline data collection $_____
Annual monitoring costs $_____
Direct Management Costs
Caretaker $_____
Property maintenance $_____
Property improvements $_____
Direct costs of administration $_____
Other:_____ $_____

Other Holding Costs
Describe any other items not covered elsewhere: $_____

_____
_____
_____

Note: Property taxes, assessments, interest, etc.,
listed above, should also be computed as holding costs.

Income from Property
Describe income possibilities, if any:

_____
_____
_____

Estimated Staff Time
Direct hours   _____
Dollars for direct hours $_____
Overhead estimate $_____

Public Agency Purchase

Basis of Public Agency Commitment to Purchase
Describe official action taken:

_____
_____
_____

Written commitment to purchase:

_____
_____
_____

Describe fiscal and political realities:

_____

_____

_____

Note alternatives, if agency defaults:

_____

_____

_____

Terms of Purchase by Public Agency
Date to be purchased _____

Purchase price to be paid by agency $_____

Other amounts to be paid by agency $_____

Date set to close _____

Project Income
Appraisal or estimate of value $_____

Other evidence of value $_____

Price acceptable to agency $_____

Potential margin in transaction $_____

Estimated land trust share of savings $_____

Costs of Closing with Public Agency

New Appraisal (if required)

Direct cost $_____

Expert Services
Attorney (to handle closing, etc.) $_____

Other consultants $_____

Direct Pre-Closing Expense with Public Agency
Telephone and postage $_____

Travel $_____

Meals and lodging $_____

Other:_____ $_____

Title Insurance
Amount to be insured $_____

Estimated premium $_____

Miscellaneous Closing Costs
Transfer tax stamps $_____

Escrow fees $_____

Reconveyance, recording, and notarial fees $_____

Other:_____ $_____

Estimated Staff Time
Direct hours _____

Dollars for direct hours $_____

Overhead estimate $_____

Bibliography

Books

Adirondack Land Trust, *Developing a Land Conservation Strategy: A Handbook for Land Trusts*, second printing. Keene Valley, NY: Adirondack Land Trust, 1989 (P.O. Box 65, Keene Valley, NY 12943).

Environmental Data Resources, *Environmental Grantmaking Foundations Directory*, Rochester, NY, 1993 (1655 Elmwood Ave., Suite 225, Rochester, NY 14620-3426).

Land Trust Alliance, *The Conservation Easement Handbook: Managing Land Conservation and Historic Preservation Easement Programs*. Washington, DC: Land Trust Alliance, 1988 (1319 F St. NW, Suite 501, Washington DC 20004-1106).

Land Trust Alliance, *Conservation Options: A Landowner's Guide*. Washington, DC: Land Trust Alliance, 1993.

Land Trust Alliance, *The Economic Benefits of Open Space*. Washington, DC: Land Trust Alliance, 1994.

Land Trust Alliance, *The Standards and Practices Guidebook: An Operating Manual for Land Trusts*. Washington, DC: Land Trust Alliance, 1993.

Land Trust Alliance and the National Trust for Historic Preservation, *Appraising Easements: Guidelines for the Valuation of Historic Preservation and Land Conservation Easements*, second edition. Washington, DC: Land Trust Alliance and National Trust for Historic Preservation, 1990.

Small, Stephen J., *Preserving Family Lands: Essential Tax Strategies for the Landowner*, second edition. Boston: Landowner Planning Center, 1992 (P.O. Box 4508, Boston, MA 02101-4508).

Periodicals

Land Trust Alliance, "Land Trusts and Hazardous Wastes," a special issue of *Exchange: The Journal of the Land Trust Alliance*, Volume 8, Number 3, Summer 1989.

Land Trust Alliance, "Land Use Planning," a special issue of *Exchange: The Journal of the Land Trust Alliance*, Volume 9, Number 4, Fall 1990.

Land Trust Alliance, "Limited Development: An Overview of an Innovative Land Protection Technique," a special issue of *Exchange: The Journal of the Land Trust Alliance*, Volume 7, Number 4, Fall 1988.

Land Trust Alliance, "Managing Conservation Lands," *Exchange: The Journal of the Land Trust Alliance*, Volume 8, Number 4, Fall 1989.

The Hyperion Society, *The Back Forty: The Newsletter of Land Conservation Law*. San Francisco: University of California, Hastings College of the Law, published bi-monthly (200 McAllister St., San Francisco, CA 94102). Covers developments in real estate, land use, taxation, and exempt organization law that affect conservation and preservation efforts.

Myers, Phyllis, *GreenSense: Financing Parks and Conservation*. San Francisco, CA: The Trust for Public Land, an occasional newsletter (116 New Montgomery St., 4th Floor, San Francisco, CA 94105). Reports on public funding to conserve distinctive natural, historic, recreational, scientific, and scenic resources.

Index